The Transforming Gift of Dreams

The Transforming Gift of Dreams

Your Dreams Are the Key to Revitalizing Your Life

Kenneth A. Schmidt MS, LMFT

ISBN: 0692703055
ISBN 13: 9780692703052
Library of Congress Control Number: 2016919361
Kenneth A. Schmidt, Ventura, CALIFORNIA

<u>**Previous Books by Kenneth A. Schmidt**</u>
Finding Your Way Home **(Regal Press, 1990)**
Promised Joy **(Winepress, 2012)**

Contents

Why Read This Book on Dreams?

The Dalai Lama said it well: "Every change of mind is first of all a change of heart." I would add, "Every change of heart is soon a change of mind." This is the urgently needed work of mature spirituality...Transformative education is not asking you to believe or disbelieve in any doctrines or dogmas. Rather it is challenging you to "Try this!" Then you will know something to be true or false for yourself.

—FATHER RICHARD ROHR FOUNDER OF THE
CENTER FOR ACTION AND CONTEMPLATION

WHY TRY THIS particular book on dreams? Why am I strongly saying, "Try this!" when there are many books on dreams available for you to read? What would make this one unique that would lead you to try it, rather than one of the others?

I have read a number of these books in preparation for writing this one. Many have valuable information about dreams; they give you ways of interpreting, analyzing, or understanding your dreams. However these approaches give people the idea that understanding something is the same as experiencing it—but that hasn't proven true. Rather, it is our experience that changes us into becoming more complete, more functional people. Academics unknowingly have taken something very simple and made it incredibly complex.

This book will not help you interpret your dreams. Instead, I will strongly encourage you to avoid doing this. It will usually be possible to understand why the dream occurred and why you had it, but only after working it through. This is often possible, but it is not the understanding that transforms you.

Instead we will be cooperating with the purpose of your dreams. Their purpose is to help you become whole, to help you live in and enjoy your world and your life. When we cooperate with their purpose, we can experience genuine, life-changing transformation. We can even experience becoming new, healthier people who are enjoying life in new ways.

> *Our deepest calling is to grow into our own authentic selfhood, whether or not it conforms to some image of who we ought to be. As we do so, we will not only find the joy that every human being seeks—we will also find our path of authentic service in the world.*
>
> **—Parker Palmer,** *Let Your Life Speak*

We are in a time of immense change, a paradigm shift, regarding our understanding of ourselves as human beings. For centuries we have viewed ourselves as creatures of the mind, meaning that our thinking and almost all our attempts at changing us or transforming us into new, healthier human beings have focused on changing our thinking. Through neuroscience, the science of the brain and nervous system, we are discovering that we are more creatures of the heart, of our emotions and feelings, our affect, rather than just our thinking. For this reason, I call this process *affective dreamwork*.

The Transforming Gift of Dreams

Certainly our thinking remains important, but when it comes to transforming ourselves into new beings who react to others and ourselves in healthier, more enjoyable ways, we must have a deeper change occur— a genuine change of heart. Now some neuroscientists even seriously consider the organ of the heart as being part of the brain rather than as a totally separate organ.

Thirty years ago, I was led to make what seemed to me to be a simple change in the way gestalt dreamwork was used in therapy. I focused deeply on the feelings, the affect, revealed by our dreams rather than trying to interpret them or make logical sense out of them.

Step by step, I discovered the power of this way of dealing with dreams. I saw people's lives change before my eyes. I loved what was happening, and, through the years, I learned more about how to use our dreams for transformation.

Over the last three years, I have been amazed to discover that laypeople can learn to do affective dreamwork, not only for their own personal healing and growth but to help others become more whole and alive.

I have seen this happen in small groups that I have taught this process to. Those who really chose to immerse themselves in it discovered themselves growing and changing in unexpected, wonderful ways. They also discovered that they could help friends and family grow by leading them through the process.

Now I know you can do it yourself. You may be so thinking oriented that you decide that you cannot make the shift to discovering your feelings. You may then conclude that this doesn't work.

But if you learn how to access your feelings and stay with the work, you will discover yourself changing without effort. Sometimes someone else will inform you of your changes, but, more often, you will discover yourself behaving in new, healthier, and more enjoyable ways and realize dreamwork's incredible power. You may even feel led to start small groups of your own using this book, and you may discover you have the ability to share and teach this process.

I am nearing the end of my life, and I trust that what I have been given will grow through people like you who are not therapists but deeply want to bring life to yourself and possibly others. Never expect yourself to be "perfect" at this, for there is no such thing. You will find your own way to incorporate what you learn into your life.

If you choose to help others with their dreams, be sure to never tell them who they are or should be, but pay loving attention to who they are at the moment. Your acceptance of them as they open up their hearts may change them forever.

Just as our muscles must relax to allow the blood to get to them to give them oxygen and life, we must relax to allow *life*, however you may believe in or express it, to have access to our fragmented, hurting parts. Dreams reveal those hurting, fragmented parts that have been hidden in the darkness without the light of love.

I want all those who are willing to face, and even relax into, their own personal pain to become healed and enjoy life more than ever before. I offer you the gift that was given to me. If you are open to entering a new world of experiences that will first change your heart, and then change your mind—to help you become who you really are, then this book is for you.

CHAPTER 1

Receiving the Gift

A mind that is stretched by
a new experience can
never go back to its old dimensions.

—OLIVER WENDELL HOLMES

WHEN I FIRST became a psychotherapist, I focused on helping people develop new ways of thinking about life and themselves, and then working with them to change their behavior to fit these new beliefs. Almost every theory of psychotherapy I was taught focused in some way on changing people's thinking in order to change how they felt and behaved. I was teaching them *about* life, not helping them *experience* it in a new way. I was teaching them that life is about learning what they should do, and then trying to do it.

This has been the paradigm, the way of understanding, that has existed for centuries. After working in this way for a few years, I met with a client who had been with me for many months. In a stressful situation, she had repeated a pattern that we had been working to change since the beginning of her therapy. She had repeated the same behavior that she'd been struggling to avoid for a long while.

She was frustrated and felt guilty for failing to do it. I, too, was frustrated, because I could see how hard she was trying and deeply wanted her to enjoy the life she had. Her husband and children loved her, but she could not truly receive their love. Trying to help her change the thinking she'd developed from childhood was not working in the way I'd been taught that it should.

Gradually, as I worked with other clients as well, I discovered that just changing our thinking has little effect on the feelings that trigger our behaviors. Doing it from the "outside in" by changing our behavior so that we'll feel and behave differently helps with some problems but doesn't create the deep emotional change we need.

I was frustrated because I could see I was only giving my clients new, healthier "laws" to believe and try to follow. Helping them reason and understand their behavior was not creating the change I hungered for and that they deeply desired. They were experiencing great difficulty because their emotions still carried them down painful, damaging paths. Without my knowing it, what they had experienced in life was still in control, despite them intellectually believing otherwise.

Becoming Who You Really Are

When we take the time to truly examine ourselves, as people in therapy choose to do, we all would like to become new, more alive people. We usually try to make this happen by thinking differently about things. Usually (and sadly), the harder we try, the more we fail. We want new life—but it seems impossible.

Our cognitive beliefs (our thinking) and our affective beliefs (our feelings) are often not the same at all! And our affective beliefs are what repeatedly and automatically take control. We need a change in heart, a change in the person we are inside, in order to truly change our minds, our thinking, and our behavior.

If you go to the core of their teachings, most religious traditions say this change has to occur first within, and then this new reality within you will change your behavior. You probably also know that the religious teachings most of us have experienced screamed the opposite message to us. They told us to "do better" or "try harder" or some subtle version of the same message. They have almost never offered us any way to do it "from the inside out."

Let me tell you the story of an event in my life that illustrates me trying to do exactly what I'm describing to you. I was leading a high-school weekend retreat in the mountains when the weather suddenly took us by surprise.

One of the teens looked out the window and yelled, "It's snowing!" Every kid in the room ran laughing out into the delightful, surprising snowfall. It was snowing—and I was the only one who wasn't happy. After working diligently to explain God's love to them throughout the evening, here was one more interruption. I ran to my car and emptied the radiator, fearing it would freeze in the unexpected cold. As I did, kids scampered around me tossing snowballs, making angels in the snow, and rejoicing.

Just as I was making an important point, the snow had shut down my lesson. Everyone left me and my truth behind. They didn't want to know how much they were loved. They just weren't getting the serious business of the theology I was teaching them! So who had the problem?

Clearly, I did!

But all of humanity is in the position I took that evening. Love and life were pouring down in the beauty of the snow, the kids were rejoicing in it, and I missed it completely. Only my agenda and my fears counted. In fact, I thought they were missing out on life because they weren't hearing what I was teaching but were enjoying life instead!

I didn't see the snow, the kids, or the love available to me. I was so busy talking about life and love that I didn't receive them. My words were good, my motives sincere, but I was blind.

Rather than being alive and aware with them, I was teaching them to be unaware and to think about life and love, even though it was present all around us before, during, and after the snowfall. I was intently teaching them about love, rather than loving them.

But isn't this just how we humans usually operate? We teach about life rather than helping others experience life in our relationships with them. Far too often, we think that life is about what we intellectually believe and try to live our beliefs out. We do that rather than experiencing life and automatically living out of genuine experiences.

I needed to more deeply experience love in my heart in order to change my thinking and my responses to the beauty of life. Big changes in my heart have occurred for me since then. (If you're interested, see my previous book *Promised Joy* for some of this story.)

When we don't know the transforming resources available to us, life is frustrating. I was yearning for more—for my clients and for myself. Then in a surprising way, through a relationship with a new client, all of this changed.

Unexpected Life

Steve began our counseling session excited and with much to tell. He had remembered three dreams and had worked through them on his own. More surprisingly, he reported a situation at work that previously would have stressed and depressed him. This time, he handled it assertively and felt a sense of accomplishment. "A few months ago, I couldn't have done that. I'm changing," he said. He was changing more rapidly and with less effort than anyone I'd ever known!

I had been a therapist for seven years when I first met Steve. When I began my training, I had been skeptical about dreamwork because it seemed weird and unscientific. I did, however, sense some value in the gestalt approach to dreams.

The Transforming Gift of Dreams

"Gestalt" is a German word that means wholeness. The gestalt approach views our dreams as revealing fragments of ourselves that need to reconciled or integrated for us to experience wholeness and new life.

Throughout my early years as a therapist, clients had sometimes shared disturbing dreams and asked if I knew anything about them. I had tentatively tried the gestalt approach with them, including some changes I made that focused on emotions and that seemed natural to me. This usually helped people, so I developed some confidence in it. I had no idea of the power that simple shift to emotions (affect) would have.

> *Affect is the most fundamental element of the mind and brain. Like the physical elements of gravity, wind and lightning, emotion has force and direction.*
>
> —*David A. S. Garfield*

Then Steve came in. Early in our therapy, Steve had a dream and asked me about it. So we tried my modification of the gestalt method, and it seemed to help. But then, to my surprise, he started using the process at home on his own, so we included it in most of our sessions. He continued changing without effort! No one had ever taken hold of the method as Steve had, nor had I ever used it for myself. He believed in it more than I did—so he was doing the growing.

Because of Steve's growth and excitement, I decided to take my dreams seriously and work through them, using the method I had devised, based on the foundation laid by Fritz Perls in his development of gestalt therapy. This is the method I will be sharing with you. I was surprised at what I discovered within myself and was amazed at the changes I knew were taking place.

My wife affirmed this when she said she could see that I was more confident and assertive in my teaching and speaking. I had made no effort to change my way of teaching; the changes were coming from within—from my heart.

After Steve had been in therapy for a few months, he came in one day and shared what he'd experienced with his dreams that week and how he was growing. As I silently listened to him, I realized that he no longer needed to be in therapy—and then, about halfway through our session, he looked at me and said, "Ken, I don't think I have to come to see you anymore." That was our final session. I tell the "rest of the story" regarding Steve in the last chapter.

Here I will simply tell you what I have learned since then, as I have worked with different clients and their dreams. As I share the steps of dreamwork, I will illustrate those steps with dreams I have been given permission to use by those who dreamed them.

You will not be able to do this entire dreamwork process all the time. I don't always do that either. But the steps reveal ways you can use your dreams so that they become a regular part of your healing and personal growth.

But first, let's think together about this. What is it about being human that creates these different "parts" of us, these "fragments," in the first place? We will focus here for a while before going into the process together. In chapter four, we will begin to focus on actually doing the dreamwork.

CHAPTER 2

Through the Eyes of Science

*Doing therapy without dream
interpretation is like
doing orthopedics without X-rays.*

—*GAYLE DELANEY*

GAYLE DELANEY EXPRESSES a confidence in dreamwork that is the equivalent
of the confidence physicians have in their use of X-rays. Delaney connects
working with dreams to the "hard sciences" of physics and medicine.
Although I will encourage you not to interpret your dreams, I completely
agree with him. Dreams open up the deepest parts of us in the same way
that X-rays do with our physical bodies.

Throughout history, many cultures have focused on dreams and tried
to make sense of them. Although almost all historical spiritual sources are
clear regarding the importance of dreams, modern science is divided and
often skeptical about them. The modern debate about dreams began after
the questions raised by the work of Sigmund Freud in the late eighteen
hundreds.

Freud assumed that dreams reveal aspects of the unconscious mind.
He postulated that there are realities about who we are and what we feel
and believe that are not accessible to us consciously; they are hidden within. According to Freud, dreams reveal, in symbolic form, what is deep

in our soul. It is like we carry an unknown "darkness" within us, which some therapists call the "shadow" part of us.

Most people consider Freud's discovery to have marked the beginning of modern psychology and psychotherapy. Since his work, other techniques have been developed to gain access to these unconscious, hidden parts of us. Hypnosis and projective testing are major tools for doing this.

The goal of hypnosis is to help individuals set aside their defenses and reveal what is deep within. In projective testing such as the Rorschach inkblot test, we're asked to share our reactions or tell stories about a picture or randomly shaped object in order to reveal hidden aspects of our personality.

Note that the stories we make up in projective testing are from pictures that we didn't create. But when we do this with dreams, we have created the pictures ourselves, so that what our imagination discovers, we can trust even more. The goal of modern dreamwork, hypnosis, and projective testing is to discover what is hidden in our unconscious minds. We know that these unconscious beliefs or emotions are motivating our behavior in ways that are invisible to us.

Psychotherapists who use these techniques discover their effectiveness and become confident in their ability to reveal valuable information about what is troubling a client. But it's hard, if not impossible, to scientifically prove that these are reliable techniques.

The biggest problem in scientifically evaluating dreamwork is its subjective nature. Hard science relies on being able to repeat results and thus predict future events. Human beings are too unique and different from one another for such repeatability to occur with dreamwork. The best we can do so far is to study the activity of the brain during dreams, and that research is occurring right now. Some of what has already been discovered about the brain is applicable to the dreamwork process.

As we explore some of this information, please understand that although I have advanced degrees in physics as well as psychotherapy, I am not a neuroscientist. Many of the recent educational conferences I have attended have focused on the discoveries of neuroscience because of its growing importance to psychotherapy. These new discoveries are changing the way psychotherapy is done. I believe that the dreamwork process I share will eventually be one of those changes.

I am definitely not saying I can "prove" that my dream process is "true." To give you an example of how I would like you to view what I'm telling you, let me share a story from my own medical history. About three years ago, I began to experience the extreme pain of multiple joint gout—the most painful form of arthritis. My rheumatologist, Dr. Pearson, prescribed allopurinol to help me, but we quickly discovered I was allergic to it.

Just at that time, the Food and Drug Administration approved a new medication, uloric, for use with gout. I really appreciated the honest way Dr. Pearson introduced the new drug to me. As he handed me my prescription, he told me that because of my science background, he was going to tell me something he seldom told his other patients. He said that using this medication was like using something from alchemy, the "science" of the middle ages. They had no idea why it worked with gout, but only that it often did. It might work, it might not, but it was worth the try and safe to use.

The uloric worked so well that I have never had any further pain from gout. It has been like a miracle drug for me and saved me hours and hours of intense, paralyzing pain. We probably still have no idea why it works, but it certainly does!

I would like you to view this dreamwork as something I know brings healing for most people and can bring new life to you. My evidence is over thirty years of experience using it with clients, followed by three years of experience teaching it to laypeople in small groups.

So what I share in this chapter is a hypothesis (an educated guess) on my part, based upon what I have learned in my limited study of neuroscience research results. I hope someone will be doing research on it in the days ahead.

I could use many new words from neuroscience to describe these processes, but I want to keep things understandable, not make them harder. I will stick to the simplest vocabulary I can use.

The Neuroscience

Each brain and nervous system consists of billions of neurons. A neuron or nerve cell is an *electrically* excitable cell that processes and transmits information through electrical and chemical signals. Neurons are connected to one another by axons, which carry electrical activity from one neuron to the next and develop electrical pathways through our bodies, especially in the area of our brains.

The connection point between neurons is called a synapse, and many of the chemicals in the medications we take today work because of the way they affect what happens at these synapses.

The statistics estimating the size of the network of neurons in a human brain are staggering. There are an estimated eighty-six billion neurons in the brain. Each individual neuron can connect with sixty to one hundred thousand other neurons so that the total number of connections is in the order of 10^{27} (ten with twenty-seven zeroes following it). This vast network of interconnected neurons is then capable of producing 10 million (ten followed by one million zeroes) possible different patterns of interconnected neurons. Based on this kind of information, it's not surprising that some scientists have labeled the human brain as possibly the most complex system in the universe.

When we experience an event, our memory of that event is stored in a connected pattern of neurons. These are identified as "differentiated parts of the nervous system." Groups of these differentiated parts represent the results of a particular experience. The firing of neurons has set up a unique pattern of neuron pathways; in short, neurons that fire together, wire together. This is how we learn.

What we have learned from an event can then be accessed by electrically reactivating that particular network of neurons. Similar experiences may cause that particular set of neurons and neuron pathways to be "fired up" electrically again. This will strengthen that differentiated set of neuron pathways and increase the likelihood that it will be fired again because it's available to help us interpret new events.

Experiments have been done in which electrical probes were used in different parts of the brain. This electrical activity would cause the person to re-experience an event from his or her past. The billions and billions of activated networks of neurons that make up our nervous system are the physical manifestation of our experiences.

Many of these neuron networks are within us at birth to make it possible for us to function, but even more are developed as we experience life. Every experience we have develops neuron pathways in our brains and nervous systems.

We know that when a baby's mother smiles at him or her, the baby's brain grows in response to that human connection. It is through interactions with people and our environment that our brains develop and grow. This is how learning occurs.

Then, when we encounter a new situation, the first thing we do is unconsciously and automatically run the information we are receiving from our senses through the pathways we already have to see if the situation is familiar. If the stimulus we've received triggers an existing neuron pathway, we use it to interpret and determine our appropriate response.

This is why it is important for parents to provide their infants and young children with a variety of stimulating experiences. Research with groups of rats confirms that those raised in more stimulating environments actually developed larger brains. The additional stimuli produce a larger system of neural networks. Each stimulus or experience either establishes a new neural path or reinforces an old one.

It is probable that the most-used paths or networks are the ones that will continue to be used in the future. Some have described this process as being like what happens when a group of people comes upon a meadow that has never been traversed. They must walk back and forth across that meadow for a period of time. The first few people who cross may take random paths, for there are no established pathways. After a while, though, individuals begin to note signs that indicate where previous walkers have traveled and will tend to follow that same path because it has been traveled before. After a time, these pathways become clearly visible to anyone passing by as dirt paths through the meadow, and then most people will use those paths to cross.

In a similar way, our childhood experiences establish neuron network patterns throughout our brains and nervous systems. When we experience a situation that seems similar to previous experiences, we will automatically use an old network path to evaluate the new experience.

This is why a veteran of battle who returns home may duck and run when a car backfires. Explosive sounds have become strongly associated with combat and danger, so the reaction comes automatically. The groups of neuron pathways in his brain are "triggered" by the explosion and lead the vet to what seem like appropriate actions but are not. Post-traumatic stress disorder can include many such now inappropriate responses that may damage the person's ability to enjoy life and relate to loved ones.

This is also the reason why children who have been physically abused automatically lifts their arms in protection when nearby adults move their arms quickly. They are accustomed to being hit, so when that movement takes place, the children anticipate that it's happening again. This is not a conscious process; it happens automatically within the system of the brain. Electrical impulses flash through the neural networks that were established by the abuse, and further abuse is anticipated.

The Transforming Gift of Dreams

This is how our nervous system "sets us up" for life. Our brains are prepared to react to external events in particular ways because these neural networks are already in place. The efficiency or health of these networks depends on what kinds of early experiences we had.

When we do dreamwork, it is crucial to know that we also have "mirror neurons" that record all of our experiences. So when your mother smiles at you, your brain records her actions, and she becomes a part of you. Your mirror neurons record her behavior and develop neuron pathways that record her behavior as your own. A part of you now exists that will lead you to behave as she behaved.

In the same way, if you are abused, the abuser becomes a part of you. This is why abused people have nightmares about being abused again. Both the victim and the abuser within the dream are parts of the dreamer. Reconciling those parts (as you will learn how to do) gradually heals the abuse.

If we were born into loving families, the networks we developed would be based on loving relationships. We would expect loving responses wherever we turned, and we would respond to others with loving responses as well.

Unfortunately, many of us received unloving responses, and the rest of us usually received responses that communicated only conditional love. This is not because our parents were "bad" parents but because the world we live in required them to conditionally love us so that we would survive. As you all know, we must behave in certain ways to be accepted, and our parents must teach us those rules, even though they may often be completely illogical.

Our survival is dependent on developing functional neuron pathways. A primary role of parenting is to develop "good enough" pathways in the child's brain so he or she will survive in the culture. These are the neural pathways, based on conditional love, that we have available, and they determine the range of interpretations and responses we have available to use.

This is why two people raised in different cultures can have a difficult marriage. Within their brains, they are very different people. Fortunately, our brains and nervous systems also have an ability called neuroplasticity—they are capable of changing. When we encounter someone with very different life experiences, we can learn new ways of responding to events through our relationship with them. For every married couple, this requires effort to make the marriage function in a healthy way.

All of us experience events that are extremely difficult to reconcile and integrate with our past life experiences. We humans regularly violate one another—we judge one another as valuable or not valuable, as "good" or as "bad," depending upon our need for what the other offers.

People in conflict "know" they are right and the other is wrong or even "know" they are "good" and the other is "bad." Countries at war always assume they are right, and the other is wrong. Our experience of these violations and judgments lead us to having neuron pathways that are not compatible with one another—and this can make it difficult or even impossible to function in healthy ways. This is where our dreams come in.

It's clear from neuroscientific research that the brain is in a unique and unusual state while dreaming. Some of the changes that take place during rapid eye movement (REM) sleep, when most dreams occur are: breathing accelerates, slows or becomes irregular; heartbeat slows or accelerates; penis or clitoris becomes engorged with blood; metabolism rises; kidneys produce less urine; brain nerve cells fire spontaneously; blood flow to the brain increases dramatically; vivid dreams occur.

This intense life experience occurs every night. Research reveals that we have seven or eight dreams per night. Even those who insist they never dream discover in research that they have been dreaming. During our lifetimes, we spend a total of five years in this state. Is anything important happening during those five years? We know that if we're deprived of the ability to dream, then we begin to have difficulty both physically and emotionally. Apparently something important is happening. But what?

The Transforming Gift of Dreams

The gestalt approach to dreams, developed by Fritz Perls, assumes that every visible object in your dream is a symbol that represents a part of you. Your dream is an attempt to reconcile these different parts of you so that they can begin working together.

So in gestalt dreamwork, we assume that the released energy and liberated sputterings come from experiences we are integrating into the whole of our being. We have so many experiences, beginning even before we were born, and our brains are working to make sense out of them all so that we can function effectively.

These will also include experiences that (1) occurred before we were capable of integrating them; (2) strongly contradicted our belief systems; (3) were expressions of ourselves that were forbidden or which we were unable to express; and (4) feelings that were too traumatic for us to absorb and "place on the right shelf" of our understanding. The sputterings and nervous energy can then be seen as a struggle to incorporate life's experiences into our souls. It is a struggle—a struggle for wholeness and understanding.

The integration of these different parts of us is a normal part of healthy functioning. We need it to survive in this world. Being able to help the process using our dreamwork is clearly a positive contribution to our health.

Let me give you a quick example of what I mean.

When Gerry was young, his father (a responsible, hard-working but somewhat withdrawn individual), greeted him in the morning with a smile and a pat on the back. Gerry's brain recorded these regular, pleasant encounters with his dad.

But when his father had been drinking, he lashed out at Gerry, sometimes hitting him and telling him he was getting in the way. These events were also recorded as memories in Gerry's brain.

Gerry's developing mind recorded both kinds of memories through thousands of connected neurons (cells in the brain) that formed complex patterns, recording each of these events. But Gerry was only two or three years old when these events happened. The pain from the times Dad hurt him could not yet be integrated with his other memories in a way that made sense out of his contradictory experiences. They were implicit (unconscious) memories. As a result, Gerry carried both these experiences within him as he married and became a father.

In his role as a father, when Gerry was with his own son, he unknowingly repeated the patterns he had experienced with his father. He genuinely cared for and loved his son but, occasionally, though he never drank, he lashed out at him, sometimes for no reason. He didn't think before he did this; he just reacted. His wife confronted him about his behavior, and Gerry began to see what he was doing and tried to change. He improved through his efforts, but it still continued to happen.

Most perspectives on human behavior that have been developed over the last 150 years or so have focused on trying to help Gerry change his thinking—his explicit, or conscious, thinking. These methods could have helped to some degree, but the change involves an ongoing struggle deeper within Gerry.

In order to naturally behave differently than he did before, Gerry has to be able to integrate his painful experience of being abused with the rest of his being. His emotional memories of being abused were stored in his brain in such a way that they were inaccessible to his intellectual understanding of his life. He cannot integrate them and become more whole until he accesses those memories and reconciles them with the rest of who he is and his understanding of himself.

This is where the wonderful work of our dreams comes in. What are our dreams all about? They usually make no logical sense, so many people (including some scientists) dismiss them as meaningless.

A POWERFUL, LIFE-CHANGING SHIFT IN PERSPECTIVE
One simple but somewhat difficult shift reveals the kind of sense our dreams make. That is the shift from thinking to feeling. As therapists

might say, we need to shift from the cognitive to the affective domain. When we shift to using our dreams to reveal what we are feeling, they make sense in a new and deeper way.

I suggest an understanding of dreams that is consistent with much of neuroscience and fits the shift I have discovered well. In his book, *The Accidental Mind*, David J. Linden considers a memory/integration model for dreams. He considers this model to be "compelling" and says that "among other things, it provides an explanation of why items in remote memory are often dredged up in dreams. They are being integrated with newer memories." This fits exactly what I have found us to be doing.

In describing REM sleep, when most dreams occur, he notes that "another striking feature of the brain in REM sleep is strong activation of regions subserving emotion." The right brain and the more primitive, emotion-laden parts of the brain are activated, so our emotional experiences and implicit, unconscious memories are strongly present.

At the same time, our left brain, which develops narratives (stories), is also active. *My hypothesis is that during our dreams, our left, narrative-producing brain is strongly connected to the emotion-recording parts of the brain, and our dreams become narratives that make little sense logically, but powerful sense emotionally.*

Dreams are about our emotions, not just our thinking, and our left narrative-producing brain "integrates the activity in these [emotion-producing] centers to produce narrative dreams with negative emotional themes."[12] My experience reveals that dreams do not often appear to contain negative emotions until the dreamwork process is done. Our brains are integrating our emotions with the rest of our understandings of life to help us become more whole and effective. To put it another way, we work to change our implicit memories into explicit ones through our dreams.

Each night, in your dreams, your brain works to take your emotional experiences and make sense of them. We must begin with our feelings and experience the dream emotionally so that we can cooperate with what the dream is working to accomplish. We are striving for wholeness within so that we can make sense of life and our world so that we can survive.

Here I will take an accepted psychological theory, gestalt dreamwork, and make one seemingly small shift in it, a focus on the feelings revealed in them. You will find that when you do this, those strange "stories" you dream make sense in a brand new way. With this simple change in focus and understanding of dreams, you will begin to cooperate with what your brain is trying to do—to make sense of your emotional experiences—but the change in thinking will occur *after* the changes in feeling.

In this book, we will be learning how Gerry can be transformed into a different person than the one who was abusing the son he loves. Doing this dreamwork process can change him within so that he is no longer abusive, without his even trying to change. The affective dreamwork process itself will change his "heart" so that his behavior changes.

But we human beings have horrendously complicated it all by the way we treat each other. This is a hard world to live in, and we have to deal with unnecessary, painful experiences even beyond what some would consider "normal." Next we'll look at what we do to one another that complicates it all.

Note

Much of what I have learned about neuroscience has come from the "Lifespan" conferences I have attended at UCLA, especially through the work of Dan Siegel, Alan Schore, and Diana Fosha, whose work and books I recommend. I also recommend the work of Regina Pally and David Olds in their book, *The Mind-Brain Relationship,* and David J. Linden's book *The Accidental Mind.*

CHAPTER 3

Becoming Aware

The child seeks adults' love because
he cannot live without it; he meets all
their demands to the extent that he
is able—for the sake of survival.

—ALICE MILLER, THE BODY NEVER LIES

AS WE'VE SEEN, in order to have their child survive in human society, parents must teach them how to be "good" according to the rules of their culture. Sadly, as Alice Miller's book, *Thou Shalt Not Be Aware*, reveals, children have to shut down their feelings in order to succeed at this. This is not a condemnation or accusation of parents because, when they were small, the same thing happened to them. This powerful effort to keep us from being truly aware of who we are lies at the core of humanity's problems.

As we saw in the last chapter, the messages we receive about ourselves in childhood and throughout our lives form the neuron pathways that exist for the rest of our lives. Sadly, sometimes tragically, what we learn can cause us to lose any awareness of who we are and how we connect with the world around us. We violate and judge one another constantly, and these judgments cause us to "shut down" parts of ourselves within the darkness of our unconscious minds. These parts in the darkness are revealed in our dreams.

Psychiatrist Carl Jung described this darkness as our "shadow self":

The shadow or "shadow aspect" may refer to (1) an unconscious aspect of the personality which the conscious ego does not identify in itself. Because one tends to reject or remain ignorant of the least desirable aspects of one's personality, the shadow is largely negative, or (2) the entirety of the unconscious, i.e., everything of which a person is not fully conscious. There are, however, positive aspects which may also remain hidden in one's shadow.

Many of the neuron pathways we develop in this judgmental world contradict one another, so we must try to integrate them to become more aware again and to become much more whole. As Thomas Merton said, we must gradually lose the "false self" the world forces us to develop and begin to trust the "true self" within every one of us. The affective dreamwork process will help you do this. Nothing is lost in this; instead, each part is reconciled and integrated to form a more smoothly functioning whole.

Just the other night, as a woman finished working through her dream, her first words were, "I feel at peace." This peace came because her heart and mind were now less "divided against themselves." Trying to change her thinking or objective reality can help to some degree, but it was the change in her feelings, her subjective reality, that transformed her. It is the same with all of us.

The problem is that the world has been forcing us to ignore our feelings in order to be "strong" enough to survive. To choose to reveal one's emotional reality can be deeply frightening for some people, so they may not want to do this dreamwork.

Our greatest difficulty is the mental resistance to things that arise, and the underlying assumption that they should not.
—Eckhart Tolle

The Transforming Gift of Dreams

This fear and difficulty is understandable because people often incur severe judgment for deep emotional honesty.

Consider how society treats people who choose to be vulnerable physically—to be naked. There is nothing "evil" about nakedness or sexuality, but we humans judge people who don't wear clothing as immoral. Anyone who violates the rules about being naked pays the price of being removed completely from others. They are considered "crazy" for their behavior.

This punishment is indeed drastic for something that was part of our enjoyment of life when we were young. Young children love running around naked. They also openly reveal their feelings without hesitation. But we teach them otherwise, often forcibly. (If my words about the innocence of being naked disturb or puzzle you, let that reveal to you how much judgment is an automatically assumed part of human culture. Why aren't the animals ashamed—and wearing clothes?)

Am I saying that we should all begin running around naked? Of course not! The world we live in would destroy us for that. Complete nakedness is extreme vulnerability.

But, recognize that, in doing this dreamwork, you choose to be emotionally open and vulnerable. This is one reason it can be difficult at first. Amazingly and powerfully, if you do this with someone who accepts and cares for you or in a group where your emotional openness is not only acceptable but rejoiced in, you will become more of your true self and be transformed step by step into the person you really are.

You will become more aware of yourself and others and discover that they are just like you. You also will discover that you are more capable of genuinely loving and respecting others than you had ever believed possible. Most religions include respect, grace, and love as part of their teachings (though the words may be different in each tradition).

Kenneth A. Schmidt MS, LMFT

Everybody is a genius. But if you judge a fish by its ability to climb a tree, it will live its whole life believing that it is stupid.
—Albert Einstein

Respect, grace, and love are the water we "fish" must live in to enjoy being who we really are—rather than struggling to be who we've been told we should be.

This dreamwork experience is one of vulnerability, honesty, reconciliation, new life, and even joy. But you must first take the risk of being vulnerable. Then the wonderful changes and freedom that are often experienced are given to you, not attained by you. All you do is to choose to be really honest and vulnerable. The rest is a gift.

As far as inner transformation is concerned,
there is nothing you can do about it.
You cannot transform yourself,
And you cannot transform your partner
Or anybody else.
All you can do is create a space for transformation to happen,
For grace and love to enter.
—Eckhart Tolle

In this new age, what Harvey Cox calls the "age of the spirit," many are writing about this in different ways and from different points of view. I am offering this process as one contribution to this amazing, positive change that is occurring. Rather than telling people who they should be, we are encouraging them to be themselves!

This change, of course, is encountering powerful, heavy-duty resistance and opposition from those who want to continue to live in the old way. They want to continue to avoid vulnerability and deep honesty so that they can use power to "shut down or destroy evil," rather than redeem it. This is what is called "redemptive violence" and is based on the idea that evil must be destroyed rather than healed and restored to wholeness—redeemed by acceptance and love.

This, of course, simply continues the pattern of judgment and violence.

To be no one but yourself when the whole world
Is trying to make you into
everyone else
Is the most difficult task
there is.

—*e. e. cummings*

Instead we need to be willing to receive and give acceptance and love in order to experience true redemption—new life. This new life opens our eyes and gives us new awareness. As our eyes open, we change—and become more capable of love and acceptance so that we then can become agents of change.

Through the years of working with people in their depths, however, I have concluded that we are not really capable of loving ourselves unless we first *receive* genuine love and acceptance. We truly cannot just "decide" to become loving; actions alone are not love. Our first step must be a willingness to open ourselves to love and receive it. Then the flow of love can begin as we gradually discover that we are beginning to love from our hearts.

This kind of love is hard, if not impossible, to find in day-to-day living. We are all so busy doing what we have to do that truly loving another often can't be fit into our agendas, even if we really want to do it. To truly love and be loved by another, you have to take the time—possibly even schedule the time—to do it. You have to be with people who genuinely want this for others and for themselves. You need an accepting, loving community.

That community might be made up of just you and one other person, such as in a therapy setting. You can do this by yourself as I do, if you decide to accept whatever comes up within you. I've discovered in the last three years, however, that a group focused on helping one another heal and grow through dreamwork is an even more powerful way to receive and give love.

We are damaged, flawed beings, and we must be loved in our imperfection. We need a place where we can be free to be as we are—imperfect. If you can accept yourself as broken and incomplete, you are ready to begin doing the dreamwork you will learn here. Let's begin.

Fundamental Steps of Dreamwork

We recognize that the truth symbols can deliver cannot be neatly pinned down. To get at it, we will have to let them dance through our imagination before they can walk into our intellects. They are telling us something, but they first speak to the heart and feelings before they can be registered in the mind and thoughts.

—Paul F. Knitter

Throughout history, truth has been told most often and probably most effectively through stories, metaphors, and parables. I suspect this is because truth cannot be effectively communicated directly. Your dreams are stories and parables about you. They reveal the state of your soul, your true self.

Dreams reveal our brokenness in that each dream symbol, whether it is a person, animal, or object, represents a part of us. Our goal is to open these parables and symbols up to "the light" so they can be reconciled to one another and create greater wholeness within us.

To say that our dreams are parables revealing the state of our inner being leaves us with a problem. How do we determine what the symbols mean? The typical image people have of dreamwork is based upon

Freudian dream interpretation. In this method of dreamwork, a therapist interprets the symbols according to certain rules of dream and symbol interpretation. Most dream books analyze the meanings of hundreds of dream symbols, based on therapeutic experience.

Effective Freudian analysis is complex. It is not something untrained individuals can successfully do with their own dreams. Carl Jung's approach also includes his meaningful views on our spiritual selves, but it is also based on interpretation according to his concept of archetypes. I am not saying that these methods don't help people, but I can no longer see interpretation as the best approach—even by a trained therapist.

My approach is based on a gestalt understanding of dreams. Every person, animal, or object in the dream symbolizes the dreamer. The symbols represent fragments of our souls that are alienated from one another—fragments that need to be reintegrated.

Working from these assumptions and assuming that the dreamer is the best source of information about the symbols leads to a less-complex process of dreamwork—a method that can be used by the dreamer for personal growth and healing. This is not an intellectual process of analyzing the dream's meaning. It is an emotional process of trusting whatever emerges within you as you "become" that symbol in your dream.

This emphasis on affect, emotion, is a shift that is taking place in psychotherapy because we now know that just changing our thinking does not truly change the power of the emotional reality within. Our feelings continue to move us in directions that are unhealthy for us unless we find a way to heal the pain we carry within.

To illustrate and explain the basic steps of our process, I will use a dream a client shared at the beginning of a crucial shift in therapy. Laurie (not her real name) had a childhood that was dominated by alienation and abuse. She never had a sense of belonging or closeness as a child. Anytime she did something "wrong" in the eyes of her mother, she'd be punished by her mother not talking to her for days. Intense anxiety brought her into therapy. She feared important people would reject and abandon her. Our work, before this dream, helped her realize intellectually that she was loved and accepted, but she still couldn't accept it emotionally.

She was just realizing that I actually liked and enjoyed her as a person. This dream marked the beginning of an intense time in her therapy. After working this dream through, she began to face her childhood issues more directly than before.

Here is her dream:

> *I had a garden. A neighbor puts a weed in it.*
> *I see him doing it.*
> *I say, "How dare you?"*
> *I feel angry.*

Note the dream's simplicity. Laurie could easily have dismissed it as insignificant. Fortunately, we'd been working for a while, and she now trusted the significance of what emerged from within her. I'll use this dream and the actual steps Laurie took in working it through to explain the steps of dreamwork.

This is a brief summary of the entire process:

1. Write down your dream. Then circle or underline every object, animal, or person you *see* in your dream. In addition, count yourself, the dreamer, as a character. People or objects that are in the dream but that you do not actually see are usually not characters.

    Assume that every person, animal and object that you actually see, plus yourself, in the dream (no matter how ridiculous or frightening) is a symbol for a part of you.

2. Go through the dream again. *Discover* your reactions and feelings by *being* each symbol, including the objects. Do not try to think

during this time, just focus on being that character and trust the feelings that bubble up from within you. If it feels like you are "making these feelings up," trust that this is what you are supposed to do at this step. Discover what emerges from within you. Write these discovered feelings down as a sequence, moving from the beginning of the dream to its end.

At this point be sure to use the appendix, "Feelings Words." It will help you discover your feelings. Use this list whenever you are trying to discover the feelings of a character. In doing this, you will often discover feelings you were unaware of. This list can also be used anytime you are in a difficult spot and want some insight and relief into what is happening within you. It can be a big help.

3. Then, after discovering the feelings of a character, *temporarily forget the dream* and explore the feelings you've discovered.

   Look down the sequence of feelings you've just revealed, and ask yourself if this sequence is something you can recognize from your waking life—a part of you now or in your past. If what comes up is painful or difficult, take the time to stay there for a while, and let yourself experience it. Doing this will gradually rob it of its power.

4. Finally, begin a dialogue among the different characters, people, and things you saw, working for frank and honest communication and reconciliation.

If you don't have time to do all the steps at one time, do any portion of the process in the order given, and it will help you grow and change. You don't have to be obsessed with your dreams. You don't have to make them your highest priority in order to benefit. The more you do, the more you'll benefit, but fit it to who you are and to your lifestyle.

The Transforming Gift of Dreams

You may recognize that these are the steps used in gestalt dreamwork, but remember that the focus is now on the feelings of the characters. This opens up a deeper sense of recognition of yourself in the dream.

Now we'll break this down in detail, using Laurie's dream as an example.

Step 1: Write down your dream, and circle or underline every object, animal, or person you see, as well as yourself. These will be considered the characters in your dream.

Example of step 1: We will underline the characters Laurie saw in her dream:

> I had a garden. A neighbor puts a weed in it.
> I see him doing it.
> I say, "How dare you?" I feel angry.

So, there are four characters in Laurie's dream: *Laurie* (the dreamer), the *garden*, the *neighbor*, and the *weed*.

Step #2: Be yourself in the dream. Then identify the feelings and attitudes that come with putting yourself in that position.

Use the emotions list in the appendix to discover and define your feelings. Emotions are the windows to our soul. We can't know ourselves or others without them. Identify your reactions and emotions during each segment of the dream.

Example of step 2: In this step, Laurie put herself back into the dream situation. She used the feelings list and worked to feel what it was like to have someone put that weed in her garden. So she began by first being

Laurie, the dreamer, and found these emotions from the feeling words list: *angry, violated, betrayed, frustrated,* and *enraged almost to the point of hatred.* These were intense feelings!

The emotions and thoughts we identify in this step occur when we put ourselves into the dream situation, even if no feelings occurred while dreaming. Usually we have no awareness of feelings during our dreams except occasionally intense fear. But the symbols and situations carry the information needed for discovering our feelings.

This idea of discovering our feelings as a character in a dream can be difficult at first, because we have so little experience in paying attention to our feelings. We usually dismiss them and start thinking instead. But remember that thinking helps us avoid being vulnerable while maintaining a sense of control over what is happening.

So to know the depths of your soul, you must pay attention to and trust the feelings and thoughts that "bubble up" from within as you try to be a person, animal, or object in the dream. People often say to me, "But I'm just making this up."

I reply by telling them, "That is exactly what you are supposed to do. We must learn to trust our imaginations to bring up images and feelings that contain truth we don't yet grasp intellectually."

When a person looks at an inkblot or a picture in projective therapy, and then tells a therapist what he or she sees, the response can only come from within the person, so it reveals important therapeutic information.

The feelings that come up from within you as you "become" a dream character are unique to you. When you trust and value them, you will discover important realities about yourself. (When you work with other people, you will realize how they feel as a character is often different from what you would have felt.) Remember that we aren't trusting whether our feelings are good but trusting that they are real and are carried within us. We're trusting that they reveal truth about us and how we have deeply experienced ourselves and life.

The Transforming Gift of Dreams

Separate from dreamwork, this step of identifying your feelings is necessary to becoming a healthily functioning human being. If it's difficult, remember that you've likely not been encouraged to know yourself. But knowing yourself is crucial to your emotional and spiritual health beyond your dreams. Don't give up if you find it difficult. You will grow in your ability to do it, and it can even become a part of daily living.

Step #3: *Forget the dream*, and focus only on the list of discovered feelings. Ask yourself if you recognize the feelings, thoughts, and attitudes revealed in step two as part of *your life* in the past or present.

This recognition may include present situations. This may also trigger childhood memories. Take adequate time for this, but don't force recognition. Meaning is found, not forced. If recognition doesn't come, don't be concerned. If a childhood memory is triggered, review the experience. Identify feelings that arise with the memory. If you desire, you may pour out your feelings to your higher power for healing this memory if it is painful.

Example of step #3: Laurie's identification with her feelings in the dream. Later, I will put the discovered feelings in vertical sequential order. Laurie reported that in her present life, the feelings of anger, violation, and rage she felt as herself in the dream, in her present life most often occurred with her husband and children. She also reported that she had felt these feelings with her mother during her childhood.

This step can be difficult for all of us. Identifying unwanted parts of ourselves can bring feelings of shame. We may hesitate to confess that they are really parts of us. Honestly owning negative, hurtful parts of our personality can only occur when we already trust that we are loved. We must know we'll not be judged for our feelings; rather, we will begin to change because we've opened them up.

...a great transformation begins when we look at our minds with curiosity and respect rather than fear and avoidance. Inviting our thoughts and feelings into awareness allows us to learn from them rather than be driven by them. We can calm them without ignoring them; we can hear their wisdom without being terrified by their screaming voices.

—Dan Siegel, Mindsight

Return to step #2 and continue. Go through each of the other characters and/or objects in the dream. Just as you did with yourself, identify the feelings, thoughts, and attitudes of each. Ask again if you can identify with these as part of your adult or childhood experience.

Again, if memories are triggered, focus on them. Open up your feelings about them. State these feelings, thoughts, and attitudes as "I messages" for each character. For instance, don't say, "The neighbor feels innocent," but, as "the neighbor," report, "I feel innocent."

Example of continuing step 2: As the underline neighbor underline putting the weed in the garden, Laurie said, *I feel careless and innocent, like a child.* When, as the neighbor, she was confronted with Laurie's words in the dream, *How dare you?* she quickly felt *vulnerable, frozen*, and *numb*. She felt like saying, *I didn't know* and felt *paralyzed*.

I was surprised by these responses because there were no clues in the dream that the neighbor had childlike feelings. If I had interpreted this dream, I would have missed this completely. The dreamer must do the feeling and identifying for him- or herself.

If you are in a group working together, once the dreamer has begun identifying feelings for a character—but not before—others may suggest feelings consistent with what has been shared already. But the dreamer is always the one who says whether a feeling fits the character or not.

Further examples of step #3: When asked if she could identify with the sequence of feeling innocent like a child, and then frozen, numb, and paralyzed, Laurie quickly responded, "Yes, I had strong feelings just like that when I got in trouble as a child. Often I had no idea I was doing anything wrong, but, all of a sudden, I was in trouble with my mother."

Notice that the sequence of feelings fit the childhood sequence accurately. We then focused on these events and feelings from childhood.

Discovering these childlike feelings of the neighbor opened the door for change in Laurie. She began to remember and re-experience her childhood feelings in a way she'd been unable to do before.

As the underline garden, Laurie said, *I'm very pretty. I have a lot of color. I like it; I like being in the sun. I have pride in myself. The weeds don't bother me.* Notice that Laurie did not directly identify any emotions with this symbol, but the emerging thoughts are packed with feelings. As we focused in on feelings, they were: *pretty, colorful, warm, pleasant, joy, and pride.*

When I asked Laurie if she could identify with being pretty, having a lot of color, enjoying the sun, and feeling good about herself as the garden did, she felt embarrassed. But then, because she had learned to be honest with me, she said, "Yes. At times I feel this way about myself, but not often. As a child, I was judged for feeling good about myself and made to feel ashamed about it."

If you knew Laurie personally, you would easily recognize that she's pretty and full of life and color. Those who know her can enjoy it, but she'd been unable to. This was a breakthrough. It was good news about who she is, but she'd been taught it was wrong to enjoy it. Her family had never noticed or acknowledged her true beauty, which prevented her from rejoicing in it.

It's marvelous to see people who have struggled with problems of horribly low self-esteem granted an image of their true beauty in a dream symbol. At first they fight against believing it's a symbol for them. But once these symbols begin, they persist in dreams until the person accepts their beauty and gifts. These positive, wonderful symbols don't occur in a person's dreams until they've recovered enough to be ready to realize their beauty. Once they come and they accept them, they change within.

As the <u>weed</u>, Laurie responded simply, *"I'm a plant. I don't feel bad about myself."* Feelings: *present, alive, OK.*

It was hard for Laurie to identify with simply feeling OK about herself. She wanted to, but it was the opposite of what she'd experienced. Often positive symbols occur when people are just beginning to express and recognize this part of themselves.

As I said before, this dream was followed by Laurie recovering the simplicity of childhood. The part of Laurie represented by the weed, a part able to accept herself as she is, would return represented by different symbols in later dreams. Each time it came closer and closer by shifting from being a plant to being a stranger, to being a friend, and eventually to being herself in a dream. As the dreams changed, she became more self-accepting in daily life. This is how needed parts gradually appear in our dreams and continue to emerge until they are accepted parts of our lives.

Step #4: After identifying with all the symbols (if that is practical), then have the characters/symbols dialogue with one another. The goal of this dialogue is reconciliation between all the parts of the dream.

It's important that you don't omit uncomfortable characters or symbols but purposely include them instead. Also be sure to remember to include what seems to be the least significant dream character because it is often crucial to healing. Be suspicious of anything that is "obviously not important," as it may be the most important part of that dream! Be frank and candid.

In dialogue, people often shift into being "nice" and hiding their true feelings and thoughts, even though they know no one else is there. When they are told that they haven't really communicated the feelings discovered earlier, they almost always say, "Oh, but I could never say that," or "That would hurt their feelings," or "It would be wrong to say that to someone."

Remember that if you have discovered something unpleasant within yourself, it will never be healed until you openly acknowledge it. Honest revelation is the path to change and wholeness. It is at the dialogue stage that people often first realize the deepest power of dreamwork. Often they literally cannot speak thoughts and feelings that they've discovered, even though they know it's only role-play.

Once they are honest in dialogue, emotions are released, and changes often come rapidly. By doing this, we break out of the ways the world has forced us to conform to expectations. When we break these internal life-suppressing rules, doors that had been closed to us for our entire lives suddenly open.

One helpful and, perhaps necessary, technique in dialogue used by Fritz Perls is placing empty chairs in a room and imagining each character or object in a different chair. In my office, the client and I assign different chairs and locations on a sofa for the different parts of their dream.

For example, with Laurie's garden dream, one chair was for Laurie, and a second was for the neighbor. Across from them, the garden was at one end of a sofa, and the weed at the other. Then Laurie began the dialogue below and moved to the appropriate position to discover what each part had to say.

Although dialogue can be done without assigning positions, using them is often a powerful part of the experience. Clients often state with surprise, "I can't believe how my emotions change as I move from chair to chair." Somehow, changing from one physical position to another can help us discover feelings. If you feel strange doing this, just stay with it. You'll develop a sense of the process and discover its power.

Most often, I do my own dreamwork dialogues in my living room using the chairs and sofa for each symbol. You don't have to physically move if you're not able, but when you can, it's best. To begin dialogue, just have any symbol express the feelings or thoughts that were revealed in the earlier steps.

Example of step 4 - Laurie's dialogue: At this point I am simply going to share the exact words in Laurie's dialogue for this dream:

> Laurie (to the neighbor): *"How dare you! Why did you do this? How could you? I want you out of here right now! I can't believe you did this!"*
> Neighbor: *"You're hurting my feelings. I don't like you talking to me like that."*
> Garden: *"Laurie, it's not a big deal. The weeds are colored green—not a big deal. It's really OK. I kind of enjoy them."*
> Weed: *"It's not a big deal. I'm a plant. I'm not a bad thing. I think I look good and add to the garden."*
> Laurie: *"OK, it's not a big deal. I feel defensive. I feel like you're ganging up on me."*
> Garden: *"We still like you, love you. We just wanted you to see that it's not a big deal to us. We're not condemning you or judging you. We want you to be a part of us. Will you do that?"* (Remember that Laurie's major issue was that she was not feeling accepted and didn't have a sense of belonging with others.)
> Laurie: *"Yes, I'll do that. Are you sure you want me to be a part of your garden?*
> Garden: *"Yeah, we're sure."*

The Transforming Gift of Dreams

Laurie (to neighbor again): *"Do you? I'm sorry."*
Neighbor: *"Are you apologizing to me?"*
Laurie: *"I don't know. Do you want me to?"*
Neighbor: *"Yes."*
Laurie: *"Will you forgive me?"*
Neighbor: *"Yes, I want you to join us."*
Laurie: *"OK."*
Laurie: (to weeds) *"How about you guys? I'm sorry for being a jerk. Are you OK with me?"*
Weeds: *"Yeah, it's OK. Don't we look great here?"*
Laurie: *"Yeah, you do look great."*

Then Laurie said the dialogue felt complete. There was nothing more to say.

In this dream, Laurie reached the point we desire with all dream dialogue—a sense of completion with all alienation reconciled. This doesn't happen often! Usually we reach dead-ends that can't be resolved in further dialogue. When this occurs, just relax, and let it be. Whatever is unfinished will recur in a later dream. It can be worked on then, until resolution occurs. Having trust in your own eventual inner transformation is important. When a dream dialogue does not result in reconciliation, the issue within it will continue within you, and you will work further on it, but from a new place of wholeness that you were not at before.

With some dreams, we may not even get around to doing all the steps. In this case, expect those dream issues to recur later in new symbolic forms. Trusting in your own healing and growth as you are actively engaged in it is often hard. But I can guarantee you that if you set it as your priority, it will occur. All you have to do is dream. The process is always going on within us, all we are doing here is cooperating with it.

We can now understand what Laurie worked through in this dream. Remember—we have absorbed into our souls whatever judgments, accusations, or neglect that have occurred to us during our lifetimes. Those attitudes and judgments from our parents hurt the most because we were most vulnerable in our youngest years.

We can see that the role Laurie played in this dream was one her mother played in Laurie's childhood. *Remember that the interpretations I am now giving are irrelevant to Laurie. The change took place in the work that was already described.* If I try to explain what I saw someone do as they work, it often makes no sense to them.

If you are in a dreams group, you may notice that everybody understands what happened, but the person who did the dialogue does not! Do not be surprised when this happens.

When Laurie, as a small child, did the innocent, careless things all children do, her mother judged and accused her. This accusing attitude became part of Laurie, and she was also accusing with the people she cared for the most—her husband and children.

Within her own soul, however, she judged and attacked herself with greater intensity than she did them. This is why in adulthood, when she really cared about a relationship, she expected the other person to reject her, so she became extremely anxious. Early in therapy, we had her check out these anxious situations with friends—she consistently found they were not feeling rejecting or negative at all. She was doing it to herself. The voice was in her head.

This illustrates what we explored in chapter three. We are the judges to be most feared. The judgments we use on others are the judgments we use on ourselves in our own souls. This is the deep spiritual meaning of Jesus's statement when he tells us not to judge, and then says, "For with the measure you use, it will be measured to you" (Luke 6:42). This constant internal judgment of herself, absorbed from her mother, was ruining Laurie's enjoyment of life.

I was surprised when the neighbor and weed were positive, needed parts of Laurie. If I had tried to interpret these symbols, I wouldn't have guessed this. In working this conflict through, she accepted the vulnerable, innocent child in her represented by both symbols. This acceptance opened new life.

I was also surprised by the quick shift in Laurie when she began dialogue. Almost immediately, she was open to the point of view of the neighbor, the weed, and the garden. This quick openness indicated the progress she had already made through earlier dreams and therapy. Usually dialogue doesn't resolve this quickly. I chose this dream because it is simple and illustrates reconciliation. When you begin dreamwork, don't expect your dialogues to work out so quickly. Laurie's quick resolution occurred because she'd faithfully worked with other dreams for a while.

Again, this intellectual discussion of what occurred with this dream was not necessary for Laurie's growth. As a therapist, I see these connections, and you may also be able to after you've worked through a dream. But if you attempt to do this rather than working through the dream emotionally, you will gain nothing and will usually be wrong. Laurie didn't need to understand this; she needed the reconciling work of owning the parts of her and working it through in dialogue. It's tempting to interpret dreams rather than face them. When we interpret rather than feel, we're trying to control the situation rather than simply and vulnerably opening ourselves up.

We wish we could always reach the point Laurie did in this dream, and the conflicts discovered resolved as quickly as hers were. When this happens, we may hope that all our work is done and we're now healed, whole, and complete. Not so. We're so damaged and far from being who we can be that we must grow and mature in receiving love throughout our lives. These times of reconciliation and healing open new life to us, but we never arrive at complete wholeness.

In Laurie's case, after accepting and reconciling the child within, she had to face the pain of childhood. She had hidden the child so deeply in the dark that she had not been aware of the pain, even though it was tearing her apart. This dream was crucial to her recovery, but it was not the endpoint of her journey. She was still realizing that she's loved and loved by others. She received this as a gift because she trusted what she discovered within and trusted in it.

This process of becoming self-aware through our dreams by discovering the feelings of the characters can be seen as a form of mindfulness. To do this, you must step outside yourself to observe your "ways of being" from a neutral point of view. Research indicates that doing this changes us internally and helps us integrate within to a healthier state. Dr. Dan Siegel of the University of California (whose concepts of interpersonal neurobiology are bearing fruit in psychotherapy) says:

> *With mindful awareness, the flow of energy and information that is our mind enters our conscious attention and we can both appreciate its contents and also come to regulate its flow in a new way. Mindful awareness...actually involves more than just simply being aware: It involves being aware of aspects of the mind itself. Instead of being on automatic and mindless, mindfulness helps us awaken, and by reflecting on the mind we are enabled to make choices and thus change becomes possible.*

I recommend his book *The Mindful Brain*, which reveals a meditative way of becoming mindful. This dreamwork engages components of the mindfulness processes that Siegel researched and discovered.

As we've seen with Laurie, when you step outside of yourself, and then discover aspects of yourself that are separated from one another so that they can then become reconciled and integrated, new life emerges, and a greater sense of peace comes with it.

Don't Think; Experience

The power of affect (feelings) to transform is enormous. Unlike other change processes, it is not gradual and cumulative, but intense and rapid.

—*Diane Fosha, The Transforming Power of Affect*

I CANNOT EMPHASIZE strongly enough the power of experiencing your dreams rather than interpreting them. Their transforming power is unlocked when we discover the affect—the emotions and feelings of the characters—rather than trying to think our way into understanding them. They simply are as you are, and their feelings reveal your feelings and the power of the memories you carry around in your darkness. Focusing on our emotions, transforms us more quickly and, usually, with little effort on our part. If you are interested in learning more or especially if you are a therapist, I strongly encourage you to read Diane Fosha's book, *The Transforming Power of Affect*. I am convinced that her approach to healing our inner brokenness will transform therapy. I hope this process of dreamwork will eventually become a part of that process as well.

Let's consider another dream to add more detail to the process of discovering your feelings.

Kenneth A. Schmidt MS, LMFT

This is Judy's dream: (characters underlined)

We're in a hotel room or house. <u>Karl</u> [a former boyfriend] is with a <u>girlfriend</u>, engaging in a business transaction. He's running around doing things. He seems very capable. I'm becoming agitated with his girlfriend, who looks like a prostitute. I point out a <u>dead body</u>. He (the body) has blue pants, a plaid shirt, and blond hair. There was blood.

Let's think a little about this dream before we explore Judy's work with it. I do this to help your understanding. I did not do it with Judy because I have learned that these explanations change nothing. We can anticipate that Judy will have to identify with a girl who looks like a prostitute and with a dead body. These identifications would seem difficult if we analyze them in advance. We could think, "Oh no, there's a part of me that's a prostitute," or "Is a part of me dead?" and scare ourselves into resisting the work we have to do.

We all have certain things we'd rather not have brought up. Please remember that there are parts of all of us that are dead. Discovering a dead body means we're ready to experience resurrecting a part we haven't had available. This is good news, not bad! I have seen this "resurrection" happen so often that I feel anticipation when someone reports a dream with a dead body in it.

Also there are ways in which we all sell ourselves to others as a prostitute does. We all live lives of pretense, hoping it will bring love. In this way, we are prostituting ourselves. As you do dreamwork, you will discover parts of you that are like the worst characters in society. Grace applies to all because in our depths, we are alike.

Recently I had to deal with someone who irritated me. Then, because of a dream, I had to face that a part of me was just like that person. In fact, he was the symbol for that part of me. I realized this as soon as I started working on the dream. I had to realize my own brokenness and need for restoration.

The Transforming Gift of Dreams

This means that when we discover a prostitute or a dead body in our dreams, we can face these images with confidence and even anticipation. We are beginning a process that will lead to new life. Listen as Judy identifies with each character in her dream. First she identifies with herself as the dreamer.

> Judy: *"As Judy, I feel respect for Karl but detached. I feel ignored by him yet caring. My other feelings are: confident, forgiving, giving, left out, loving, on edge, guilty, responsible, sad, withdrawn, resigned, and pleased that we're being cordial. My feelings as Judy toward the girlfriend are superficially cordial but, underneath, feeling agitated at and judging of her promiscuous appearance. As I become aware of the dead body, I feel shocked, surprised, grief, gloomy, frantic, nervous, powerless, sorry, suspicious (I feel Karl knows), uncertain, uneasy, and vulnerable."*

When the dreamer comes to the point of identifying with the sequence of revealed feelings, I recommend putting all the feelings into sequence as they occurred in the dream, revealed in a vertical line, as I've done in my example below. You want to try to identify with the feelings, not with the reasons you felt them in the dream. The reasons supplied by the dream are simply there to reveal all the feelings, and that is what we must focus upon. (Note: I won't always be using the vertical format in this book, but I strongly recommend it for your individual work.)

It is important to report the sequence of feelings as they occur during the events in the dream. Any one event may lead to a number of feelings by itself, but write these down as you discover them, and then go on to report the ones that occur for the next portion of the dream. This vertical sequence of feelings can then be fed back to the dreamer doing the work, or, if you are doing the dream on your own, you can leave the dream, and then go down the complete list of feelings to discover if you know this sequence of feelings in your own life.

If you are working with another, then have the person close his or her eyes if desired and just listen to the feelings as you read them back in sequence.

JUDY'S FEELINGS IN THE DREAM

being with Karl:	*respect*
	detached
	ignored
	caring
	confident
	pleased
	cordial
	forgiving
	giving
	left out
	loving
	on edge
	guilty
	responsible
	sad
	withdrawn
with girlfriend:	*superficially cordial*
	agitated
	judging
seeing dead body:	*shocked*
	surprised
	grief
	gloomy
	frantic
	nervous

The Transforming Gift of Dreams

powerless
sorry
suspicious
uncertain
vulnerable

I then asked Judy if she could step out of the dream and identify with these feelings as a part of her life. After I read the feelings to her in the order they occurred in the dream, she said she actually felt these feelings with Karl, but that they were also feelings she had regarding her father during her teen years. She felt ignored and left out of his life, although she was trying to be loving, forgiving, and giving to him. When this didn't bring the love she desired, she became sad, withdrawn, and depressed. She felt responsible for his rejection of her, although she had no idea what she'd done wrong.

Then we moved on to identifying with Karl.

KARL'S FEELINGS

at the beginning:	*busy*
	competent
about Judy:	*aware*
	glad
	determined
	respectful
	in control
	detached
	trapped
	accepted
	fun
	proving myself

	protective
	capable
about the body:	*puzzled*
	ignoring

When I read these back to her and asked her to identify with this whole sequence of feelings, Judy quickly responded, "Yes, I don't want to give time and attention to things. I want to deny problems exist. I overlook them, keep busy, and hope they'll go away."

The next step was to identify with the girlfriend. Judy had trouble getting started, so I asked her to begin by physically describing herself as the girlfriend. I recommend this as a helpful step whenever someone feels "stuck" in discovering the feelings of a character or symbol. This can be especially helpful with objects. She began with a physical description, and then the feelings came quickly.

Girlfriend: *"I have brown hair and a tight-knit blue blouse and black high heels. I feel used, but I'm accepting it and allowing it. I feel I'm in control if I'm allowing it. I don't feel vulnerable, and we have fun. I'm protecting myself, and it gives me something to do. I have little feeling but, instead, feel detached. I don't really know the man I'm with."*

THE GIRLFRIEND'S FEELINGS

used

accepting

allowing

in control

not vulnerable

self-protective

active

fun

The Transforming Gift of Dreams

unfeeling
detached
disconnected

Judy said she didn't see the body when she was being the girlfriend. If she felt that she could see it, we would have included her feelings when she viewed the body.

When asked if she could identify with these feelings, Judy remembered that this was the way she'd been as a teenager. She became involved with drugs and promiscuous sex. This was a difficult identification because it caused her shame. Always give dreamers the option of not sharing their identification if they would rather not.

Finally, I asked her to identify her feelings or thoughts as the dead body. When individuals first do dreamwork, they often react with surprise at being asked to do this. "How can I identify with a dead body? They're just dead; there's nothing to identify with." When I get this response, I encourage them to try it and see what happens. If nothing comes, that's OK. In this case, once Judy started, these feelings came:

Dead body's feelings:

ignored
questioning
abandoned
forsaken
uncared for
frustrated
indignant
panicky
angry
ashamed

avoidant

uncared for

helpless

When asked if she could identify with these feelings, she replied that it was difficult, and she was unsure. She couldn't quite make the identification. I didn't press it, assuming that when she was ready, she would do so.

Judy began her next therapy session with these words, "I'm feeling depressed. I'm wasting my life and feeling defeated. I'm feeling dead." I reminded her of the previous week's dreamwork and asked if she felt these feelings now. She replied that they fit accurately. The dreamwork revealed Judy's feelings even before she was consciously aware of them!

At this point, I could have explained her dream to her if I had so chosen. Don't bother to do this when working with another person unless asked—and only after the person has finished working through the dream. Remember that you are not a therapist, and don't step into telling people what to do or otherwise acting as if you are. Please only do the work that I am describing to you.

For your benefit, I'll share what I saw in her as she identified with the feelings revealed in each character.

Throughout her childhood, Judy felt ignored and left out by her father. She tried to deal with this by being extra loving, giving, and forgiving with him as most children do. She felt guilty because she thought she must have done something wrong to cause this rejection. Eventually she became resigned and withdrawn and gave up hope regarding her dad. If you go back, you'll see that these were the feelings Judy had as she identified with herself in the dream.

When she gave up in her attempts to please Dad in hopes of getting his love, a part of her died emotionally. If she hadn't shut these feelings down, she would have felt ignored, left alone, uncared for, helpless, angry, panicky, and ashamed. She concluded that she was worthless and left out of her father's life. If you review the feelings revealed by identifying with the dead body, you'll see these fit.

During her teens, she gave up trying to please father and turned to drugs and sex to find acceptance. She allowed boys she didn't know to use her. This gave her a sense of controlling relationships with men. Emotionally detached, she was going through the motions of life just to have something to do. These feelings fit those revealed as she identified with the girl who looked like a prostitute, and they are the feelings that lead most prostitutes to sell their bodies.

The Karl part is easiest to understand. As she emerged from her teens, she took on the role of a responsible, busy adult. She was so busy that it was obvious she was occupying herself to avoid facing her feelings. She kept doing things and ignored problems. Much of her therapy had focused on slowing her down so that she could pay attention to who she was.

When Judy finished working through this dream, doing the other steps as described before, I could have shared all this interpretation as I've written it. Surprisingly, almost every time I share an interpretation like this, the person can't quite grasp it. Months later, Judy was able to accept and agree with the interpretation I've just shared, but it would have been of little help at the time of the dream. Yet the work she had done, plus the dialogue that emerged from it, created changes in emotion and behavior.

She recognized ways in which she allowed men to use her now. She recognized the deadness in her present life and began to face pain that had troubled her for years. The change occurred even though she could not intellectually understand it at the time. Again, the intellectual understanding follows the emotional change, not the other way around.

Please remember this as you do your own dreamwork. You may be the last person to recognize that you are changing because it will flow without effort. After a while, people will report that they sense you've changed. You may discover yourself doing things you've never been able to do. Something has been healed within. It is a gift. Receive it as such.

Kenneth A. Schmidt MS, LMFT

In summary, I encourage you to consider each of the following as you do steps one through three in dreamwork:

1. *Put yourself in the physical and relational position of the symbol you are identifying with and simply pay attention to and trust whatever emerges from within as you do this.*

     Begin by physically being in the dream as that symbol. The physical is important in accessing our emotions. Brain research reveals that our emotions are not just in our brains, but also in our bodies. After working to physically be the symbol, feel yourself in the relationship(s) the dream reveals. Judy had to feel herself being with Karl for the feelings to emerge. Try to set aside any evaluation or judgment, and just be. Trust what emerges as having value, and record it. Use "I statements" to state what comes up.

     When you are discovering the feelings of a character other than yourself as the dreamer, be careful that you don't inadvertently assign feelings to that character based upon what you see as the dreamer. If you see what appears to be a happy, attractive character, you might say he or she feels happy and attractive. But when you become that character instead, you may feel sad and misunderstood. You must first *become* that character to discover the feelings.

2. *If nothing comes spontaneously, slowly go through an emotions list. Identify all the feelings that seem fitting or even words that stand out, even if you're not sure you feel them.*

     I've discovered that the words that stand out usually have meaning. For whatever reason, we're not ready to feel those emotions. Frequently when dialogue starts, they become important. State these in the form, "I feel..." as much as possible. Be alert to not saying "The dead body feels..." but rather, "As the dead body, I feel..."

If you can't get started, take time to describe yourself physically *as* that symbol, whether it's a person, animal, or object. Do not describe the symbol as you see it as the dreamer. Describe yourself as the person or object you are being. As you give this description, pay attention to any feelings or thoughts that emerge, and record these.

Again, the physical often holds clues to the emotional. Describing ourselves as the symbols somehow helps get us into those positions in the dream, and this triggers feelings. For example, if you're being a car, you might begin by saying, "I'm a small red sports car. I may be a convertible." This physical description may trigger further responses such as, "I'm designed for fun, and I'd like to be out on the road." Your subconscious mind has chosen the symbol to represent what you discover when you do this. Trust these responses even if they seem contradictory to your "normal" sense of self.

3. *Don't let the foolishness or seeming insignificance of being a dead body or an object block you from identifying with it. After a while, this feeling will evaporate because you'll discover that the feelings arising from these images are valid.*

4. *If you identify with a person, animal, or object and no feelings come, assume that absence of feeling is what that symbol represents, and record it. Don't assume this when you first begin doing dreamwork because you may have not yet allowed yourself to discover your feelings.*

 Symbols may stand for a part of us that is emotionally dead. Identifying with that will open the door to further recovery in later dreams.

5. *When you get to step two and try to identify the discovered feelings, thoughts, or attitudes as part of yourself at some point in your waking life, also check if the feelings fit how you felt with your parents as a child.*

Most of our emotions began in childhood when our ability to feel them was developing. Even if you identify with the feelings as an adult, check to see if they are also true for you as a child. Often, our adult reactions were formed in childhood. In our groups, we've often discovered that this is important.

We often, if not usually, live our adult lives by continuing to create circumstances that lead to those same feelings! Freud noticed this and labeled it "repetition compulsion." This may seem unbelievable to you, but therapists see this on a regular basis with their clients, so don't neglect this possibility.

6. *Take some time to explore your feelings from any memories that arise.*

    Review the situation or situations you've remembered. What were your feelings then? How did you respond? How do you wish you'd been able to respond?

7. *If you cannot identify with a character's feelings as a part of you, ask yourself if the feelings would fit a significant person in your life as a child. They may be the feelings of your father, mother, or sibling.*

    Remember that the mirror neurons in our brains result in our absorbing the people and events in our experiences into our own being. You may have absorbed the feelings that have arisen from another rather than their initially being your own. For this reason, it is important to say a clear "No" when you try to identify a part of you that had the feelings revealed, but you cannot. They may be feelings that were demonstrated frequently by a member of your family rather than feelings you personally experienced.

    Saying "No" then opens up the question, "Was there someone in your childhood who you believe lived with this set of feelings?" You may have absorbed that person's feelings into your own being.

    If a character feels angry, critical, mean, hateful, and attacking, you may have had an abusive parent who displayed those feelings to you with great intensity. You have absorbed them into yourself, and, until this part is integrated with your healthier parts, it will continue to treat you abusively from within. This internal self-abuse makes it impossible for you to feel good about who you are, no matter how hard or long you try. When the abusive part is reconciled and integrated within, the self-abuse ends.

8. *If you can't identify with the feelings you discover and they just don't fit any significant person in your past, don't worry. Just assume that identification will come later.*

   When someone reports that they can't identify with feelings or attitudes, they are often able to do so within a few weeks. Don't turn anything in dreamwork into a "should." It's an experience of grace and redemption (new life). Your part is simply to show up, to be open to the process, and to stay honest.

CHAPTER 6

Dialogue and Reconciliation

*We are a mass of contradictions
longing to be reconciled.*

—FATHER RICHARD ROHR

MATT WAS GOING through hell. He'd just lost his job and now seemed to be losing his wife. She was separating from him. He'd been in therapy for a long while, recovering from a childhood without love. Now, just as his outward life was falling apart, he was coming alive within. He was beginning to feel.

So far, most of his feelings had been negative. He felt abandoned, rejected, and unloved. Most of us would share these feelings in his circumstances, but, for Matt, they weren't new. They'd been present all his life. Just a few minutes into our session, he commented, "I don't have any idea what it's like to feel loved."

This was no exaggeration. He had experienced neglect almost from birth, abuse from his "friends" in school, and his previous marriage ended in divorce. That day, he shared this dream (characters underlined):

> _Marge_ (Matt's wife) was lying in bed. _I_ came into the room with her, and we reconciled.

We had no idea if such a reconciliation would take place. We couldn't assume the dream was a message from God predicting that they would reconcile.

The Transforming Gift of Dreams

These were Matt's feelings as himself in the dream: excited, anticipating, warm, affectionate, reconciled, close, and connected. As Marge in the dream, he reported the same feelings.

You might wonder, "Why even bother to dialogue two parts feeling this good about each other?" Listen to the conversation between these characters as we move into the next dream step of dialogue—you'll see.

Matt: *"I feel excited, warm inside. I feel we're connecting—real love, healing. It feels good. I want to hold you, and it feels good. It's real. I know you mean it."*
Marge: *"I love you. I accept you. I want to love you and accept you as you are. I have warm feelings of love and acceptance for you just the way you are."*
Matt: *"Those are words I've always wanted to hear. At last no one is trying to change me."* (Tears flowed with these words.)

I wish you could have been there. Matt is a muscular, masculine young man. To see him vulnerable, receiving and experiencing love was a beautiful moment. Now he knew what it felt like to be loved—he'd experienced it in a dream!

Months of honest confession had laid the foundation, and now, during the worst time in his life, he experienced love. Speaking these feelings and hearing them spoken to him helped Matt experience the new reality he was being given. This is the reason for doing dialogue, even when a dream is positive. These enjoyable dreams are signs of healing and new life. In dialogue we "solidify" these feelings and experiences deep into our souls.

Speaking the words makes a difference. Most scientists and philosophers identify the crucial distinction between man and animals as being our use of language. Recent brain research emphasizes this.

We use language not only for communication, it also affects the development of our brain. We are creatures of communication. The primary characteristic of dysfunctional relationships is poor communication revealed in dishonesty, avoiding emotions, and denying reality.

Honest communication is crucial for healthy relationships between man and wife, parent and child, and between friends. It's also fundamental to our personal mental health. We are constantly communicating within ourselves.

> *Mental health is an ongoing process of dedication to reality at all costs.*
>
> *—M. Scott Peck*

If this internal dialogue is honest and based on reality, we face life responsibly and effectively. If not, we're headed for trouble. You will discover that your dreamwork dialogues are conversations you have within your own mind. Speaking the dialogues aloud brings us face to face with our internal alienation and brokenness, as we'll see in our next dream.

This is a dream of Charles:

> *I was on some kind of safari or expedition in Africa. As we emerged from a group of trees, we came upon a pack of hyenas that killed and began devouring a <u>young deer</u>. I particularly noticed <u>one hyena</u> that seemed to be most violently devouring it.*

He found the hyenas repugnant and distasteful. He hated everything they represented. As we worked, he saw the hyenas (a symbol subconsciously chosen from a nature show the night before) as ugly, self-centered, cowardly, and attacking the weak. These were not the feelings of the hyenas, but Charles's description of them. (You must be careful not to confuse your feelings *about* a character with the feelings *of* the character. They are usually not at all the same.)

The Transforming Gift of Dreams

The issues that brought him into therapy were spousal abuse and an impending divorce. When asked to identify a part of him that would attack the weak, he resisted. The shame over his abusiveness and anger overwhelmed him; he avoided discussing it. We had discussed his father's abuse of him as a child, and he consistently defended him by saying, "Well, I had it coming. I needed it. I'm a better man because of it."

Most of his earlier dreams had signs of violence in them, but it was always "off screen." The figures who acted violently did not appear in the dream, but the results did. This was his first dream that portrayed a figure acting violently. If I try to force people to deal with negative, hurtful parts of themselves prematurely, they can't do it. Their dreams reveal this inability—no symbols representing this part will occur. The appearance of this symbol revealed that Charles was ready to face his violent behavior.

The hyenas had attacked a young deer, a fawn. We first worked through the symbol of the deer.

Step #1 feelings as the deer: *weak, terrified, vulnerable, overwhelmed, destroyed, devastated.*

Step #2 identification with those feelings: *This is hard, but I flashed on the times my dad used his belt on me. Sometimes I was afraid he was going to kill me. He was so angry.*

Now Charles could remember his vulnerability and pain as a child being beaten by his father. Next, I asked him to identify with the aggressor, the one doing the damage.

Step #1: feelings as the hyenas: *angry, powerful, hungry, attacking, dominating, in control.*

Step #2: identification with those feelings: *"This was my father when he was hitting me."*

After discussing how this fit his father, I reminded Charles that our goal was for him to discover *a part of him* that was like this.

After resisting, hesitating, and reacting as I revealed earlier, he replied, *"I just can't say it. It's too painful. I never wanted to be like my dad, but now I find myself accused of doing the same things he did to me. Yes, damn it, I am like the hyena. When I get stressed, something snaps, and I lose control. I hate this. I don't want it to be true. I feel like this when I lose my temper with my wife. It's like something has taken me over completely and the rage just pours out of me. Then I feel disgusted with myself for what I've done."*

This honest confession initiated Charles's deepest healing.

For dreamwork to be effective, we must dedicate ourselves to revealing reality at all costs. This was difficult for Charles, and it will be difficult for you and me to face a reality we hate; we might wish it would go away. But as long as we don't face it, it never goes away! In fact, unless we face our negative realities, they become stronger and control our lives even more. In dreamwork, we must face reality, first, when we're asked to identify with a character's emotions and thoughts as part of us. Then, it requires our facing reality as we are in dialogue.

People often do the first dreamwork steps honestly, and then when asked to begin dialogue, slip into pretending and being nice. For instance, if a dream character has revealed a hatred for another person, dialogue may begin with something innocuous like, "Hello. How are you?" It's not quite that far from the truth, but close.

When I say, "Wait a minute; a little while ago you said you hate this person, and now you're acting like your friends. Why not tell the truth?"

They respond with, "But I can't just come out and say I hate them. That wouldn't be right."

The other person really isn't there, so why not tell the truth? For some it's incredibly difficult to speak boldly even when no one will be hurt! This reveals the power of dialogue for changing us. It requires us to face and work through feelings and attitudes we may intensely avoid.

If you want freedom from negative thoughts and attitudes, then be honest in your dreamwork. If not dealt with, the feelings you hide will eventually damage relationships. This is why Charles's honesty was good news. I knew that after honestly confessing his abusiveness, it would lose its power. He was no longer hiding it from himself.

Evil is characterized by the uncanny game of hide-and-seek in the obscurity of the soul, in which it, the single human soul, evades itself, avoids itself, hides from itself.

Martin Buber

If family rules taught you to be nice rather than truthful, you'll have trouble with dialogue. This mindset damages our ability to be in relationships, because we can't communicate our most painful thoughts and feelings. But it's an amazing discovery to find out how healing, love, and life come through honesty. We often believe "niceness" will fix things, but it leaves everybody frustrated and in pain—and no one knows why. Niceness that hides the truth leaves pain unattended and, with time, destroys us.

Here are Charles's feelings in his "hyena dream"

Step #1 Feelings as Charles: *shocked, disturbed, unsettled, upset, angry, hate, disgusted.*

Step #2 identification with the feelings (identifying how those feelings fit your real life): *"Yes, I can't stand seeing these kinds of scenes in movies and on TV. Somehow they really disturb me."*

Working through Charles's dream required him to reclaim two lost parts. First, he had to re-own the weak, hurting child he had left behind in childhood (because it was too painful). Then he had to own the harsh, abusive part of him that he had experienced and absorbed from his father.

Since that time, Charles had never allowed himself to be vulnerable again. It was too scary. His childlike vulnerability and spontaneity were beaten into the darkness by his father's abuse. In identifying with the fawn, he began recovering the child within. This helped him relate to his wife and children by revealing his weaknesses and difficulties.

He also reclaimed the strong, abusive part of himself. Sadly, when people try to disown a strong, abusive part, they not only avoid being abusive, but they also give up their strength. That abusive part does not disappear, however; it then comes out unexpectedly and is out of our control. This is what had been happening for Charles with his wife.

Except for his abusive episodes, Charles lived passively and was never truly present with others. His childhood survival depended on not revealing weakness or demonstrating strength. For Charles and most abused people, strength and abuse seem linked and inseparable. Those who didn't experience loving strength are so often unable to be strong without being abusive.

In doing his dreamwork, Charles didn't take long to recognize the hyena as being like his father. Fortunately, he moved beyond that and found it in himself as well. He was deeply ashamed of this because he didn't want to be like his father. Under stress, however, this took over, and he was abusive. Afterward, he felt guilty and ashamed and returned to trying to be good.

This pattern had existed for years. He couldn't acknowledge his strength or his weakness. Now he was confessing them both through one dream. When Charles eventually reconciled his needed strength with his hurting child within, he was able to be strong without being abusive. This dream was only the beginning.

For dialogue to take place, first choose the point in the dream to use. With Charles's dream, we had two choices. We could dialogue either when the hyenas were first attacking the fawn or after the fawn was killed. We chose the beginning of the attack. We agreed that the two chairs in my office would be the locations of the hyenas and deer. The sofa was Charles's location.

I asked Charles to say to the hyenas or fawn whatever he wanted to say. *"Stop it! Stop it now! You have no right to do this to that defenseless creature."*

> Hyenas: *"Who are you to be talking to me like that? Watch out, or you'll be my next dinner. I'll do what I want when I want."*
> Charles: *"You ugly thing! I hate everything about you. You're cowardly and evil. I wish I could stop you."*
> Hyenas: *"But you can't. And I couldn't care less what you think of me."*

At this point, Charles turned and said, *"That's all there is. I can't make him stop."*

Now I encouraged him to speak to the fawn.

Charles: *"I'm sorry. I can't stop him. I wish I could."*

Fawn: Charles sat in the fawn's chair and said, *"It's too late. The fawn can't respond."*

Reconciliation was not achieved in this dialogue. I asked if the fawn could speak to the hyena. Charles tried this—then he replied, *No, he's just too scared.* This absence of resolution typifies dialogues when a new part of the dreamer has been revealed. Reconciliation seldom occurs at first. Occasionally alienation is so complete that dialogue can't even begin.

When "stuckness" occurs, take the conversation as far as you can. If it ends and you can go no further, just stop. If you have a partner helping you, and you desire help, you can ask for a suggested next step. Don't force this. If you stop prematurely, the issues will pick up in a later dream. Don't put yourself under pressure to succeed. Just do it honestly, at a comfortable pace.

As Charles continued to grow, new dreams brought the abusive part closer and closer. In a later dream, rather than observing abuse, he was the person being abused. Still later, he was the abuser. These gradual steps from one dream (or group of dreams) to the next are how we proceed in owning a shameful or frightening part. That part first appears as a distant object or person, and then occupies a more central dream role, and finally we experience it as the main character. We can seldom own and integrate it within one dream or in one dreamwork session.

Charles was still recovering when he moved away. By using dreamwork, he never had to attack or blame his father. We discussed what had happened, and he faced his feelings of abuse, but therapy never degenerated into blaming his parents.

Blaming is a dead end. It caused our problems in the first place. It avoids personal responsibility and focuses on another's failings. Since we're all fallen and imperfect, blame just continues the tragedy. Charles eventually confronted and discussed the abuse with his father, but he didn't attack him. By responsibly doing this and entrusting his healing to his higher power, he stopped the cycle of blame.

Shame Keeps Us Apart

What makes it hard for us to face reality? Shame. Shame prevents us from living honestly because we're afraid to reveal who we are. We're convinced we won't be accepted. But if we break through the shame, reconciliation is possible.

To illustrate this, I'll share another one of my own dreams. I originally worked this through as a dialogue demonstration in a seminar, so I transcribed it from the tape. You may recognize issues revealed in my wolf dream described later in chapter seven.

The Dream:

The Transforming Gift of Dreams

I'm in a room across from a <u>coach</u>. He's sitting in a chair with his head down, and he's not looking at me. I sense he's disapproving of my job and I decide to get a different job to try to please him. (Chair and room are not visible.)

This is the work I did with this dream:

Step 1 feelings as Ken: I feel *disapproved of, rejected, wanting to connect and not being successful.*

Step 2 identification with Ken's feelings: "*Yes. I always had a subtle feeling that my dad had no real interest in what I was doing and that he might disapprove.*"

Step 3 feelings as the coach: "*I feel detached. I'll not look at him. I have power, but I'm passive and not really alive.*"

Identification with coach's feelings: "*Yes. For a long while, I struggled with being detached and distant from men.*"

Dialogue:

> Ken: "*I feel disapproval. You don't approve of me or like what I've done with my life. I feel that you don't care about me.*"
> Coach (hardly any feelings): "*I don't know why you feel that way. I don't have much response to what you said.*"
> Ken: "*Auugghh! I'm frustrated! I'm here! Can you see me? I feel like shaking you to bring you back to life. I want to know you're present with me and that you see me!*"
> Coach: "*What are you so upset about? Keep your cool.*"
> Ken (At this point I've become aware that the feelings I'm having relate to my father): "*I'm your son! I want to know you know who I am and that you care about me. I feel hurt that I haven't gotten to know you,*

and you haven't gotten to know me. I want you to pay attention to me and see me!"

Coach (looking up): *"I don't know how to do that. I don't know how to know you. I don't know how to let you know me. I've never experienced that in my life, so I don't know how to give it to you. I'm sorry."*

Ken: *"That feels good. It feels good to hear you talk to and acknowledge me. Thank you. It's OK if you don't know because now you're looking at me and acknowledging me. How do you feel about what I'm doing with my life? What's it like to see me?"*

Coach: *"Ken, I'm proud of you. I appreciate what you're doing. It's beyond me. I don't really understand what you're doing, but I'm proud of you. I appreciate what you're accomplishing."*

Ken: *"Thank you. I feel loved."*

It's important to note that this was an issue I was working through in my own soul. Before my father died, we had had a conversation like this in which he communicated his positive feelings about me.

Even though the issues were no longer present with my father, they were still giving me trouble within. It is important to remember that the unreconciled issues within you, especially involving parents, often stem from childhood pain. The pain may still be present even though the adult relationship has become a positive one.

It's also critical to notice the words that began the reconciliation. When the coach said, "I don't know how to do this," everything shifted. He broke through the shame. This happens frequently in the dialogues of clients as they deal with frustrations with parents. Shame keeps parents from telling their kids they don't know how to do something.

It's especially hard to say, "I don't know how to love you." We judge ourselves and assume we should know how to love. But when we give our children honest answers, relationship begins. Giving honest answers is loving. In saying we don't know how to love, we are loving. As we confess we don't know how to relate, we're relating. Getting past the shame of who we "should" be to simply being who we are is the secret for healthy living.

Facing Reality Clarifies Our Beliefs

Sometimes facing reality requires us to rethink our beliefs. We discover we've misused or misunderstood something because we thought it was what our higher power desired. The following dream illustrates this. The person who shared it was a young Christian woman, whom I'll call Kari, who was working hard to live the life God desired. Kari was experiencing a lack of joy and said, *"There's a block in my life. I feel in bondage, with only glimpses of freedom. I can't find a church I feel right about."* Here is her dream:

> An evil <u>man</u> is trying to attack <u>me</u>. This is not a sexual attack, but he meant harm. He kept tickling and poking me, and it hurt. I couldn't get away. I held the <u>Bible</u> up. He tried to grab the middle pages, but he couldn't rip them. He went down on the ground, writhing. I catapulted to the ceiling. He was repelled; I was pushed up. Then I was in a strange, dreary <u>theater</u> with other people who had fought in similar ways. I'm avoiding <u>dog piles</u> in <u>sand</u> in the theater.

As she worked through the dream she first identified her feelings as Kari:

Step #1 Kari: *"While being poked, I feel intense, strong fear; helplessness; a little hurt; maybe violated, but not sure; and trapped. While holding the Bible up, I feel uncertain, yet hoping. When he grabs it, I'm afraid he'll tear the pages out. As I open it fully and shove it in his face and I'm floating, I feel determination, making a last-ditch effort, struggling, and then relief and surprise. As I'm sitting in the theater and have a sense that I'm avoiding dog piles in sand, I feel amused, but also eerie. I'm asking why am I here and experiencing no joy or life? I don't want to be here."*

Her sequence of feelings: *strong fear, helplessness, hurt, violated, trapped, uncertain, hopeful, determined, giving effort, trying, struggling, relieved, surprised, avoidant, amused, eerie, questioning, joyless, lifeless, wanting to escape.*

If we "interpreted" the dream at this point, we might conclude that Kari's Christian walk was helping her prevent abuse and violation. As I listened, I was anticipating that this would affirm her faith in the Bible and her Christian lifestyle. This seemed true when I asked if she could identify with the feelings she discovered as Kari.

Step #2 identification with Kari's feelings: *"They remind me of conflicts with my ex-husband and a time when bullies locked me in a closet during elementary school."* These were the times she felt violated. Then things took an unexpected turn.

Step #3 She discovered her feelings as the man:
Feelings as man: *tired, fed up, forced, avoidant, strongly wanting to escape.*

I was surprised by these feelings, as I had expected more forceful, violating feelings from what seemed like an aggressive character. My expectations were wrong! It was crucial that I went with her feelings, rather than my own, as that character.
Then she identified with these feelings as part of her real life:

Identification: *"Yes, this is how I feel about life now. I'm tired, feel the Bible is being used against me. When I go to church too often, I feel the things some people are forcing on me are like the dog piles in the sand, and I've got to avoid them. I don't want to be there."*

We almost missed a crucial object in this dream, but then I remembered to have Kari identify with the feelings of the Bible.

Bible: *"I'm being forced on someone. I'm becoming a barrier between people."*

Identification with feelings as the Bible: When asked to identify with this, she realized that her own attempts to force Christian beliefs on others had this effect. She felt she was becoming a "barrier between people" rather than loving them.

As we moved to dialogue, the issues became clearer. (These are the actual words she spoke! I am not making this up.)

Dialogue:

Kari: *"I'm so afraid. I'm afraid you're going to violate me. You can't do this to me. It's not fair. It's not fair for you to force yourself on me. I feel helpless."*

Man: *"I can't live this perfect life you're trying to force on me! Would you please stop? I feel exhausted but relieved to have finally said this."*

Kari: *"I don't want to admit I've been doing that. It means I'm not perfect. I'm afraid of not being perfect, of being wrong. Intellectually, I know otherwise, but I'm afraid of condemnation. I'm really afraid of letting the Lord's light shine in. I fear you'll expose my imperfections. I was using the Bible in the wrong way."*

Man: *"I can't get free. You won't let me get free. I can't get free to be who I'm created to be. I'm living under bondage. I can't live up to your standards. I can't live up to your fear of doing something wrong—your standards of perfection."*

Kari: *"I'd like to let you. I don't know how. I want to live as Christ did. I don't. I'd like us to become one. I want to set you free."*

Man: *"I feel frightened. I might get what I want. The walls of bondage wouldn't be around me anymore. I'm feeling exhilarated but also a little wanting to stay in bondage. At least I know what it brings…but I don't want to stay in it! I like your strength and determination. I would like you to use it to help get me free."*

Kari: *"I like your spontaneity, love of life, and joy. I see it as risky and threatening, but I've always been jealous of it. I'd like you to use that to help set me free from the lack of luster in my life—my incredible soberness."*

Now the Bible was brought into the dialogue:

Man (to the Bible): *"I've been condemned by you for being spontaneous, fun, and free, yet the Christ I've read about gives us that freedom. I feel I've had to change my behavior because I didn't act like I'd been baptized in lemon juice. I couldn't live up to what people said I should be."*

Bible: *"My words were never meant to be used that way. I'm sorry."*

Kari (to the Bible): *"I've tried to live up to your expectations, and I couldn't. I tried to act Christian, but, inside, I was still empty. But I kept persevering. I knew you were true and for me. I'm sorry I used you in a way you weren't meant to be used, but thank you for taking me through some barren places."*

I hope you can feel the wonderful wholeness that came from this dialogue. Facing reality and speaking it candidly helped Kari enjoy a part of her created by her higher power. This was the childlike spontaneity revealed in the man who, at first, seemed evil and dangerous.

Those things we fear the most are often gifts we've been given. When Kari finished, the responsible part of her was still there, along with the Bible-believing part. But now a childlike part was available as well.

Nothing good within her had been lost, and all had found their proper places in her soul. These are the blessings of dealing with reality even when it seems threatening.

Summary

Summarizing the basic things to keep in mind as you dialogue:

1. *Assign chairs or room locations for each dream symbol. Go to these locations before responding as that symbol. You will discover these locations help trigger your responses.*
2. *Choose a place in the dream in which conversation between symbols seems most possible. Remember that dialogue is conversation that you continue from the dream; it is not conversation that occurred during it. The dream sets up the situation, and (by doing the steps listed earlier) reveals the feelings it represents. The dialogue is what you do to resolve the conflict in the dream. If you don't feel drawn to a particular part of the dream, then start at the beginning.*
3. *As you assume the position for that symbol or character, speak whatever flows out of you. Remember that this is confession, so this is not the time to edit your words to avoid saying "bad things." Be honest! honest! honest!*
4. *If you feel stuck, then go back to the emotions you discovered in steps one and two. Speak these emotions vulnerably to the other symbols. Remember this vulnerability is what creates change.*
5. *As you dialogue, don't neglect any dream symbols. Sometimes one symbol breaks the deadlock between the others. When you first do this (or when a dream is complex), it may be necessary to simply choose two or three main characters for dialogue and ignore the others. Just do what you're able to do at the time.*
6. *If you sense a character is taking action instead of speaking, let the action occur in your imagination. These actions are usually important and create*

essential change. Events in imagery change things within us. Our imagination was created by the spirit just as any other part of our being was.

7. If you become stuck and have a helper, ask if you are missing anything obvious. This is the main help another person can give. Often the most obvious things are invisible to us, because we've never been allowed to see them!

8. If a character wants to leave the room and not talk, remind yourself that this is a part of you. Ultimately you can't ever leave or get rid of it. However, if leaving is all that part can do, go ahead. It will return in a later dream anyway, but when it returns it will be changed, and you'll be able to take new steps that are impossible now.

9. If you are in a dialogue that seems like an unresolved one your parents had or one you've had with them, you'll be tempted to stop where it always stalled. When this happens, remind yourself that this isn't your parents, but a part of you. You can go past this point and experience a reconciliation they never achieved. For example, if your parents always argued about money and never agreed, you may discover yourself arguing about money in a dialogue. If you persist in being honest and vulnerable (which your parents probably weren't), you can resolve this within and change your experience.

10. Stay with dialogue until you're sure it's stuck or it is reconciled. If you decide it's stuck and you can't continue, stop, and don't worry about it.

When we speak the truth and work to listen, we grow. Dialoguing is a process of trusting whatever emerges and speaking it frankly. As you do this with dreams, you'll discover that you do it more effectively every day. As you grow, you'll discover a new ability to speak the truth in love that wasn't there before.

CHAPTER 7

Discovering Treasures Within

*The most repressed and denied aspects
of our soul...are often the treasure
that lies buried in the darkness.*

—CARL JUNG

JULIE'S DREAM WAS a bundle of confused images and events dominated by pain and alienation. As she identified with the symbols that revealed hurt, she had little difficulty owning the feelings as her own. She was familiar with feeling lost and confused, as the main character did. She recognized the hurt of rejection revealed by an object tossed aside. Then we came to an object that threw her completely. It was a gracefully shaped porcelain vase.

As she "became" the vase, these were her words, *"I'm beautiful and delicate. My features are carefully crafted and pleasing to touch. I am very feminine and yet somehow strong."* She shared these reactions and seemed fairly comfortable and confident in their accuracy as the feelings of the vase. Then I asked the same question I had asked with every other symbol, but this time it caught her off-guard. After reading the feelings back to her I asked, "Can you identify with these feelings as true for you?"

For a moment, Julie's eyes glistened. Then she abruptly blurted out, *"No way, that's not me. I wish it could be true, but there's no way I can identify with that."*

Kenneth A. Schmidt MS, LMFT

Sitting across from me was a beautiful young woman whose features were delicate and whose skin was silky smooth. She had experienced so much family trauma that she had needed strength simply to survive. Her words describing the vase fit her well. Yet when asked to own these marvelous feelings as true of her, a struggle began.

The dreams we had already worked on were filled with hurt and neglect. She had spent weeks grieving, was getting stronger, and her depression was lifting. This beautiful vase was the first positive image in her dreams. When this moment happens in someone's recovery, I become excited because I know I am now participating in something wonderful.

But that first healthy image of beauty is so difficult to acknowledge. People fight against believing they could be that beautiful or loved—the brief glisten of tears was the only acknowledgement that Julie could give of this first revelation of her as a beautiful creation.

When this happens, though I know good things are coming, I must be patient while the person struggles to accept the good news. Even though this first positive image may be rejected, other positive images will follow in other dreams.

Gradually, step by step, the person realizes personal beauty and loveliness. As this happens, he or she experiences life in a new way. The person begins to discover the treasure hidden in the darkness.

This example reveals how important it is to discover the emotions and attitudes revealed by each symbol *before* you attempt identification. If I had asked Julie straight out, "Are you in any way like the vase in your dream?" the answer would have been a quick denial or an intellectual response analyzing the meaning of the vase, and we wouldn't have had that brief moment of recognition revealed by the glisten of pain and hope in her eyes. The vase's meaning could only be revealed truly by discovering the feelings it symbolized. It's important to rigidly stay with the dream at this first point in dreamwork.

The Transforming Gift of Dreams

For many of us, trying to identify the feelings of someone or something in a dream seems so strange and difficult that we feel incapable of it. We are so busy "editing" our thoughts and feelings to eliminate those that "shouldn't be there" that we're unaware of what's inside us. These initial steps require reassurance that whatever we discover is OK, that it's common to all of us and can be opened up. We are breaking through the barrier of shame that prevents us from knowing ourselves.

How do we begin? We begin by knowing that we are acceptable and lovable just as we are. This foundation must exist before we can safely converse about the uncomfortable broken parts of who we are.

We must feel completely safe from judgment or rejection if transformation is to occur. Believing that someone will accept you without judgment may prove difficult for some, but accepting this offer of love is vital. Some may draw on their faith to ground them in recognizing their being loved and accepted in their imperfections. Others may need to trust in the mystery of the dreamwork and let it play out as it will.

It is being discovered that *mirroring* is a process that leads to transformation. This means that you have an opportunity to see yourself as you are as if looking into a mirror.

This is an excellent way to view your dreams. They reveal to you a number of mirrors in which you can see yourself. Every single character in your dream is a mirror image of a part of you. Our emotions reveal the *being* of that part of us, and, by first taking the time to discover how that character feels, we have a chance to become aware of that part of us as if looking in a mirror. That dialogue then gives us a chance to have those parts become reconciled and integrated.

As you do your dreamwork, remember that the dreams reveal the *present state* of your emotional and spiritual self. They are not yet the deeper truth about us, but we must release these revealed self-perceptions by openly acknowledging them and owning their reality as ours in order for us to gradually experience the new reality.

Kenneth A. Schmidt MS, LMFT

To further illustrate the discovery of treasure hidden in the darkness, I'll share a dream that represented a turning point in my life. Years ago I went to a men's conference in Phoenix, Arizona. The conference helped me understand a sense of frustration and emptiness that had haunted me since my teens.

For the first time, I recognized my passiveness and my lack of power and vitality. I returned home, gathered a group of men for a weekend retreat, and shared what I had learned.

From that weekend, and with the support of the men in that first workshop, I developed and led a series of men's retreats and became part of a group of men who planned, developed, and led such retreats together for a number of years. All of this began with a dream that was a turning point in my feelings about myself as a man. (I have underlined the characters.)

> I'm the <u>lead rider</u> of three men (I see <u>man number two</u>) on horseback, riding toward a <u>campsite</u> with a burning <u>campfire</u>. As we ride into camp, I'm aware of a <u>wolf</u> rushing down the mountain on the other side of the fire. I know he's coming straight into our camp. I reach down and pull my <u>rifle</u> from my saddle. As the wolf runs into the camp, I shoot him in the hip. He falls to the ground, writhing in pain.

When I began work on this dream, I had no inkling of what was to emerge from it. As I identified the feelings of myself as the lead rider, I felt: *in charge, responsible, good, superior, competent, above it all, and unthreatened.* These feelings were easy to identify, but unpleasant to confess. This had been my way of living since I was a little boy. If you have a sense that this rider was wearing a white hat, you've gotten the idea.

I'd spent my life being good, strong, and in control. I'd been a "good boy" and grown up to be a "good guy." Notice that I felt no vulnerability whatsoever. I was good, competent, and "right," but essentially unfeeling.

The Transforming Gift of Dreams

This part of me was not truly alive. (I share why this was "me" in the book *Promised Joy*.)

As I shifted to being the wolf, I tried to feel myself running down the mountain. At this point something happened that surprised me. If I had tried to interpret the meaning of the wolf, I would have guessed that he was mean and destructive. When I became the wolf, something entirely different emerged. I never had a chance to look at the emotions list because it hit me so strongly: *"I am your power. I'm not coming to hurt you. I'm coming to lead."* As these words flashed into my mind, I felt the power and rush of energy as I roared down the mountain. Then came the flash of the rifle. *"No, don't do this to me. You need me."* Then I felt *wounded* and *crippled*.

The wolf's sequence of feelings:
powerful
wanting to lead
energetic
alive
wounded
crippled

When I tried to identify with these feelings, I easily recognized feeling wounded and crippled. I had felt a lack of power and vitality during my adult years. The rush of power the wolf felt coming down the mountain was new. I had always judged power as a "bad" thing, so I'd never expressed it. Now, I loved it and hoped it could be mine. Even as I write, emotion flows in me because of the gift of that power.

When I became the second rider, I discovered that I was asleep in the saddle. The only feelings I could muster were: *unaware* and *out of it*. Again, these feelings were easy to identify with, but very unpleasant. I had spent most of my life being passive. I was hesitant to lead or make things happen. As a husband and father, I had followed or resisted my wife's lead rather than leading. This passiveness was something I first recognized at the Phoenix conference, although I'd seen it in other men many times. Until this time, I could never really own it as my own.

I won't do the other characters now but will move on to share the crux of my experience with this dream.

When I moved to dialogue, here's what happened:

Wolf (to the lead rider): *"I am your power. I've not come to harm you or anyone. I'm here to lead."*

When I heard this as the lead rider, I decided to holster my rifle and not shoot the wolf. Notice that I had a physical response to the dialogue, rather than a verbal one. This happens occasionally.

Dialogue is the interaction between the symbols that flows once you have them communicate with one another. Just trust whatever flows from within when you begin the dialogue. In this case, I sensed what happened next. I *experienced* it as I saw the wolf and riders in my imagination.

As soon as the wolf realized he would not be shot, he ran to the second rider, jumped up, and grabbed him by the belt with his teeth, and then pulled him from the saddle. He shook him to awaken him. As that second rider, I gradually came alive, but with little energy or clarity. (Most of your dreamwork will not be as "active" as this one was for me.)

Dreams will often seem meaningless when you first discover them. Please do not dismiss them. You will discover their relevance when you get into the feelings of the characters.

As we look back at this dream, we can see that the powerful part of me that I had been afraid of for years was no longer being held back by "good Ken" but had been trusted and allowed to act in freedom. They had been reconciled.

That day, after working through this dream in the morning, it occurred to me that a local talk show might be interested in having a guest who would speak about men's issues. I seldom had thoughts like this—and never acted on them when I did. This time, to my own surprise, I picked up the phone, phoned the station, and told them my idea. They phoned me back a little while later and arranged for me to be on their show. I had never been on radio, was nervous about doing it, but was still able to act in a powerful way.

For years, my wife had told me that my speaking could have greater conviction and energy. I knew she was right, but could do nothing to change my style. Since this dream, my wife commented on the change in my conviction and presentation. I had been given a valuable gift—and all I did was "be" the characters and allow them to honestly interact. I see this kind of change happen on a regular basis using this process.

Back to the Neuroscience

The earlier "meadow crossing" metaphor can help us understand what is happening in our brains when reconciliation occurs. Again, I am not a neuroscientist, so this is hypothesis, even though I'm convinced of its truth.

Earlier we thought of people crossing a meadow as a metaphor for how our neural pathways are developed and strengthened. They are used until they become strong, and then are used over and over—even when they are not necessarily healthy for us.

An example is the combat veteran who ducked for cover when he heard a car backfire. He had developed necessary neural pathways that were effective for combat situations that were still automatically used when his senses received input that resembled an explosion or a gunshot. They were needed and healthy in combat, but a detriment in peacetime.

The neural pathways developed during our early experiences may have been helpful for healthy relationships or not. Regardless we tend to repeat those same reactions and attitudes throughout our lives.

To some degree, all of us have learned many unhealthy, damaging patterns that we keep living, because they are all we have. We are not aware of any options. The good news is that our nervous systems demonstrate *neuroplasticity*—they are capable of change.

Again however, in order to change our pathways, we must have new experiences, not just new thinking. When emotional parts of us become reconciled in the dialogue of dreamwork, that is the first new experience that opens the door for further similar experiences to follow.

It is as if different people had tried to cross a large meadow to get to the other side. On one side there is food and, on the other side, is water. Both are essential. If we were not given a successful way to cross that meadow during childhood, then we have only developed paths into the meadow that lead us to something less than what we need. But they are all we have, so we keep going down those paths over and over throughout our frustrated lives (repetition compulsion).

When, however, two or more characters are reconciled during dialogue, it is akin to discovering that the old pathways can be connected in a way we had not considered possible before because they had never been an option! When two characters reconcile, it is like suddenly finding that two previously developed pathways can be connected through a new opening. Once that opening is found, the old pathways can be used along with this new opening.

These new paths through the meadow (new neuron pathways) are then used over and over and become our primary way of getting through the meadow to get to both the food and the water.

In our lives outside of dreamwork, we do this all the time—an encounter with a person who genuinely loves us; being in a group that is truly caring; developing a relationship with an attentive, concerned therapist. These can give us new experiences as can many other life situations.

The Transforming Gift of Dreams

That first discovery of the "hole," that first reconciliation, does not necessarily bring any awareness that something new has happened. But, over the next two or three months, as the individual starts to unconsciously use this new pathway, it grows stronger and stronger, and the person gradually becomes aware of the change.

CHAPTER 8

A Series of Healing Dreams

*Like emotion, healing too is also gaining
scientific respectability: We are starting
to understand that healing is a process
with its own characteristic phenomena
and mechanisms, one that needs to
be elucidated in its own right—and
that emotions are at the core of it.*

—*DIANE FOSHA*

PEOPLE ENTER THERAPY because they're under pressure; something has forced them into the open with their problems. They would like a quick fix, but that's seldom possible. If they have courage and stick with it, they mature—but this takes time.

Consider dreamwork to be the centerpiece of an ongoing healing process for your growth and enjoyment of life. Love will change you if you don't escape your pain and if you will let grace work within you. If you expect overnight change on a regular basis, you'll be disappointed—and yet, significant long-lasting transformation does occur over time. You will know it when you look back and discover ways in which you're thinking and behaving differently. You may wonder, "When did this happen?" You did not make it happen, but your willingness to be emotionally open and honest allowed it to occur.

The Transforming Gift of Dreams

Scott Peck said that grace works like a platform we're resting on that tilts in the direction of wholeness. Slowly, over time, we gently slide toward wholeness because of the "tilt" love has placed in our lives. With dreamwork, this tilt may be dramatic at times, but, as with most of life, it usually happens gradually and often out of our awareness.

In this chapter, I'd like to share one person's gradual growth to greater maturity. You will see changes occurring from one dream to the next, and, when we look back, you'll see the healing but won't be able to tell exactly when or how it happened. I share this dream series in the hope that you will let this experience do similar work in you.

Brian is a middle-aged man with a young family. He's been successful financially and, by all worldly evaluations, is doing well, yet he's coming for therapy. He's successful and takes his personal faith seriously, but something's wrong. Life isn't fulfilling; instead, it's a blur of productivity, effort, and frustration. He has no time for family and friends and no time for play. Passion and vitality have been missing for as long as he can remember. He wants more life and wants to be present in his relationships—especially with his wife and children. He's become aware of the darkness he is in and wants more light.

Even before we've begun dreamwork, Brian states that he feels divided inside. Part of him wants to relax, be laid back, and enjoy life. Another part must work hard to be successful. This division began with his childhood desire to paint. He loved oil paints and creating colorful canvases but was told to be an attorney because he could never make a living as a painter. Now he resents the responsibilities of life. As he looks back, he feels, "I got robbed."

The questions presented by Brian's therapy are, "Can the inner conflict in Brian be resolved? Can a successful career man and a suppressed, passionate artist exist together?"

Below is Brian's first dream. (Again, I will underline the characters Brian sees in the dream as I write it out for you.)

My karate <u>coach</u> is talking to <u>me</u> about karate, but his words seem out of character. He's a traditional and highly-disciplined coach, but he's telling me, "Hey, unwind."

An individual's reported therapeutic issues often appear in the first dream. I suspect you may see the connections between this dream and Brian's frustration with life. If you can't, don't worry about it because, once again, intellectual understanding is not our goal. Brian understood his problem intellectually long before he came to see me. But our goal is emotional and spiritual transformation—a new experience of life.

As you've seen before, the first step with this dreamwork is to identify the feelings represented by each symbol, using the feelings list.

As Brian began by being himself in the dream, he reported these emotions: *amazed, surprised, confused, puzzled, uncertain, and anxious.*

When I asked him to forget the dream for the moment and see if he could identify this set of feelings alone as part of himself, either in daily life or from the past, he quickly reported that these feelings were what brought him into therapy. He'd neglected part of himself for years and was surprised when it troubled him.

Now I asked Brian to "be" the karate coach in the dream. As the coach, he felt *self-disciplined, focused, and distant.* At the same time, he reported he was "*wanting change, trapped in a role I'm playing, wanting to be different and encouraging.*"

When I asked if he could forget the dream and identify with these feelings, he quickly said, "Yes, it's another way of saying what brought me in here. I want to change and experience life differently."

The Transforming Gift of Dreams

The dialogue was short:

> Brian: *"How can you be saying that? This doesn't fit your image."*
> Coach: *"Whatever happens, I'm letting a part of me be seen that normally I'd keep hidden."*
> Brian: *"That's OK with me."*

After just these three sentences of dialogue, Brian said there was nothing more either had to say. They were in agreement. Brian was ready to accept a part of him he'd been holding back for years. The pressures of life had forced these issues into the open, and the dream had simply revealed it. Though these characters quickly agreed in dialogue, one thing to keep in mind is that even when the characters in a dream don't agree, the communication between these parts has begun. This is the beginning of their integration, which will continue within you.

Now let's move to Brian's second dream—a similar theme in a very short dream:

> Mary [his wife] and I are at a costume party. People are wearing lots of outrageous costumes.

(Note: Mary was only sensed by Brian, but she was not visible, so she is not a character.)

When I asked Brian to be himself in this dream, this emerged: "I'm asking, 'How do I fit in here? I feel completely out of place. I'm a spectator and not a participant. I'm just watching.'" His feelings then were: *out of place, questioning, looking on, not participating, observing.* When asked if he could identify with these feelings as part of his life he said, "That's how I feel in so much of life. I feel out of place, as if I'm not quite present and looking on rather than truly being involved."

When asked to be the people in his dream he responded, "I don't care what this looks like. I'm part of the party. I may look ridiculous, but that's OK." So his feelings were: *unconcerned, present, aware, having fun, OK, and belonging.* When asked to identify with these feelings as part of him, he had trouble. "I'd like to be more like this, but it's certainly not a part of me I experience very often."

A new part of Brian emerged in this dream. The karate coach hinted at it, but now it's clearer. When a new part appears in a dream, it usually precedes the person's awareness that he or she is changing.

The appearance of the costumed partygoers indicated something new was happening in Brian, but he hadn't yet realized he was changing; the first reaction to a new emerging part is lack of recognition or ownership. Don't force it; simply trust the process. The new part will continue to emerge and grow.

The dialogue was, again, very short:

Brian: *"You look like you're having fun. But don't you feel awfully silly?"*
Partygoer: *"Maybe so. But you're right—I'm having fun because I just don't care if I look silly or not. Come on, join us."*
Brian: *"No way. I'm just not ready to do that. I'd feel too silly. I do feel a little envious though."*

Brian said the dialogue was complete, and we ran out of time in our session. It might have gone further, but its essence was complete. Notice the differences between Brian and the partygoer remained, but they're connecting in a positive way.

At Brian's next session, he reported a "sense of feeling better and life getting back to normal." It was getting back to the way it had been. At this point, if our focus was solely on Brian's symptoms, we would have stopped therapy. The symptoms that brought Brian in seemed to be gone after two dreams. Was the underlying problem solved? I'll let you answer that as you read his next dream. I will underline the characters as before.

I'm walking without any purpose or direction toward a nondescript, abandoned old shack in the middle of nowhere. As I walk toward the shack, another guy of about my age approaches me. He seems to be in good shape. I sense he'll attack me. We begin with verbal sparring. He attacks me physically. He's hitting me. I defend myself. Then the dream shifts to me beating him terribly. He keeps getting back up, with no marks on him. I think, "Nobody takes shots like this." I hit harder. He's up again, blocking my way. I pick up a board. I've got to finish him off. I'm whacking him. Beating him! I sense it's too much and feel remorse for what I'm doing, but then he's up again! He's invincible. I'm tired of beating him. I'll have to kill him—but, instead, I walk away.

As Brian was himself in this dream (step one) he first felt *alone, aware, apprehensive, not threatened, stalked, jabbed.* Then as the guy started sparring with him, he felt *defensive*, not aggressive. Then as the intensity went up he felt *aggressive*, "I won't be a pushover; won't back down" increasing to *confident, strong, not aware of getting hit, and anxious.* As the guy kept popping back up, he felt *amazed, surprised, fatigued, frustrated, and threatened* because "I'm giving it all I've got."

Brian's feelings (in vertical format and in sequence):

walking: *alone*
see guy: *aware*
                 apprehensive
                 unthreatened
                 stalked
                 jabbed

sparring:	*defensive*
	fairly calm
intensity up:	*irritated*
	aggressive
	resisting
	stubborn
	confident
	strong
	unfeeling
	yet anxious
popping up:	*amazed*
	surprised
	intense
	fatigued
	frustrated
	threatened

In identifying with how this sequence of feelings might fit outside the dream and in his real life (step two) he said, "*This feels like life. I keep working to be free financially and in my profession, but I always must fight one more battle. And the issues keep coming back, and I've got to fight some more. I give everything I have, and something always pops back up.*"

Next he focused on being the "other guy" in the dream. Words came quickly, without even focusing on emotions. *We had unexpectedly shifted into dialogue, but it happened so quickly and was so intense, I let it go.*

Guy: "*I'm over here; acknowledge me! You're in my turf. You're not paying attention. You'll have to confront me sooner or later. This is it. Now you can't ignore me. I demand respect. I'll show you what happens when you ignore me. I'll not go away. Deal with me! I'll push you. This will be a fight. Your shots don't hurt. Is that your best? That was better. That was good, but I'm back. You're getting stronger, but you'll have to kill me. You almost got me, close—but I'll not go away. You've beaten me for now, but I'll be around.*

The guy's feelings:

violated

ignored

disrespected

resistant

rebellious

confronted

determined

defensive

unaggressive

holding my own: *impervious*

determined

undefeated

Though the outside of Brian was looking fine, inside, the hard-working Brian was beating down the unhappy part. During this session, he remembered that a number of years before, during a time of incredible crisis, he dreamed of being chased by someone who wanted to kill him.

Fortunately, he was in a new place now, but the problem remained unresolved. When asked whether the feelings of the guy were part of him, he responded, *"Yes. This is the part of me that wants to be acknowledged, the part I've been ignoring for years."*

Further dialogue between the characters in the dream flowed after this:

Brian: *"I don't want anything. I'm just walking through. I'll mind my own business. Just keep your distance. What's the big deal? This doesn't appear to be worth fighting for. Be careful with me; I'm warning you. If you're gonna push me, you're gonna pay a price."*

Guy: *"What are you doing here? This is my patch, and you're not acknowledging me. I deserve some respect. You're going to acknowledge me and learn to respect me. You think my place is insignificant, but I'll fight for it."*

Brian: *"I don't want to challenge you. What's the big deal? I'm not threatening you."*

Guy: *"It's not that you'll take anything. You're going to respect me. I'll shove you. This isn't going to be easy. I'll not go away. Here I am. You'll have to do better. I'm not out. Why don't I fight back? So you'll respect me because I don't fight back."*

Brian: *"You're right. I'm impressed. I do respect you. But I don't understand why you're fighting over this place that has no value."*

Guy: *"It's not the place, it's the respect! That's the value.*

Brian reported that the dialogue had ended. There was nothing more to say. So we stopped.

He explained that he had problems confronting someone who judged or violated him. It didn't seem possible to confront the violation and call the violator to responsibility. Instead he remained passive, kept taking it and "coming back up" in the face of abuse, hoping to eventually earn respect. This was extremely stressful but happened frequently. Remember, any conflict discovered in a dream is one that is ongoing, unconsciously, inside of you.

So far we've neglected an important part of the dream, the shack itself. (The board was not visible.) Houses are important symbols. They often reveal the state of a person's soul. We'll discuss this more later. But for now, watch the condition of the houses that appear in Brian's dreams. This first one he described as a shack. When asked to be this shack, and reveal how he felt, he said:

The Transforming Gift of Dreams

Shack: *"I may be abandoned, but I'm still stable. I have a good roof and walls. I'll be around a long time. My foundation is solid, but there is not a lot inside. I'm dark and run-down, but I'm still in pretty good shape and in a nice location. No one is taking care of me. Neither one of you [Brian and the other guy] has any ownership of me. This is my place, and I don't want to ask anything of them."*

Shack's feelings (in order):

> *abandoned*
> *stable*
> *good boundaries* (important)
> *solid foundation*
> *dark*
> *run-down*
> *good shape*
> *good situation*
> *uncared for*
> *independent*

When asked to step out of the dream and identify with these feelings as part of him, he said, *"Yes I'm still in pretty good shape, but I've been neglecting my true self for eighteen years."* Usually when a person shares the feelings of a house or building, I will also ask them to check the condition of its foundation. I didn't do this with Brian's shack because he already mentioned it, but I do recommend asking about it. The condition of the foundation is a critical clue to how the individual feels about his or her stability in life.

We could have dialogued Brian, the guy, and the shack, but we ran out of time. This dream and the work Brian did reveal the internal conflict in his soul, his true self, as he began therapy. When we finish Brian's last dream, we'll compare it to this one.

Here is Brian's next dream:

> *I'm on a main street that runs through the center of a small town. I'm walking down the street, past retail businesses. I see a guy loading motorcycles in front of a building. It's my building.*
>
> *I confront him. "What are you doing here again?" I tell him to come inside. We go up to the second floor and begin to fight. I'm beating him but having no impact. I clobber him, but he's never intimidated. I dominated in the fight.*
>
> *He leaves with three people who watched the fight. This included two guys and a striking, nice-looking girl. She glared at me when they leave, like she's thinking, "You're a bad human being." The building is in better shape than the shack was, but it's abandoned. It's dusty with a big wooden stable and it's easily functional."*

BRIAN'S SEQUENCE OF FEELINGS

walking through town:	*relaxed*
seeing the guy:	*bothered*
	possessive
	disturbed
	secure
	aggressive
	not angry
speaking:	*confronted*
fighting:	*necessity*
	finishing off
	dominating
	strong
	unfinished

The Transforming Gift of Dreams

	unconcerned
girl is looking on:	*judged*
	puzzled

When asked to identify with this set of reactions he said, "Yes, this is my present attitude toward life and my situation. I'm under control." He didn't report any awareness of feeling judged about it.

As the "other guy" in the dream, he reported:

loading motorcycle:	*casual*
	busy
	within my rights
	respectful
confronted by Brian:	*on the spot*
	no choice
	undisturbed
	surprised at my calm
the girl is there:	*connected somehow*
more fighting:	*unending*
	no choice
	necessary
	resigned
	matter of fact

In identifying with this, Brian reported that he felt like this in dealing with life issues. There was never any resolution. He was referring to difficulties he had with attitudes of bigotry, unhealthy sexuality, and foul language. He was constantly fighting these issues without resolution. Notice how the dreamwork opened up troubling issues that had never been identified as goals of therapy when we began.

GIRL'S FEELINGS:

surprised

uncertain

puzzled

questioning

sympathetic

angry

condemning

accusing

judging

In identifying with these feelings, he said these were feelings he had toward himself regarding his bigotry, intolerance, anger, and foul language with his children. They also fit his unfeeling sexual responses. He didn't like the way he was living. He was hurting people and didn't want to continue.

Notice that this is the first time a female appeared in his dreams. This is a significant shift. Later, this part of him is instrumental in resolving his problems. I also asked him to report his feelings as the other guys looking on during the fight.

OTHER GUYS' FEELINGS:

unnecessary

dutiful

committed

disconnected

In identifying with these, Brian said this fit his passivity—the feelings he stated earlier about being a spectator rather than a participant. Notice that this passivity, which had been the predominant set of feelings in his second dream of the party, is now relegated to minor figures in the background. The internal struggle represented by the fight is now the central focus, and we now have a part, the girl, that doesn't understand the fight and disapproves of it. She becomes the central figure in the dialogue.

Girl (to Brian): *"What's the purpose of all this? Why are you handling it this way? You hurt him, why? It seems like a selfish thing to do."*

Brian: *"It seems like there's no other way. You haven't seen the whole thing. You're coming in late. Who are you to him anyway? Why should I feel accountable to you? I feel resigned. This is just the way it is."*

Girl: *"There probably are other ways. You're too caught up in routine to try to recognize them. This seems like a hurtful way, with no progress."*

Brian: *"I know there are better ways. You're right. I deserve the glare. This is not who I am all the time. I'd like you to know me beyond what you've seen."*

Girl: *"My loyalties are to him. I'm following him."*

Brian: *"I feel misunderstood. You don't really know me."*

Girl (to the guy): *"What are you going to do about this in the future?"*

Guy: *"This is done. I'll confront it when we intersect again. You don't know the background. This is a male way of handling things. It's not a big deal."*

Girl: *"Are you going to keep letting him do this to you?"*

Guy: *"It's over for now. Let's go. I'm not hurt, and I'm not worried about it. It's just something I live with."*

Girl: *"I feel like I'm walking in the middle. What's the issue? What is the fight all about?"*

Guy: *"I don't feel accountable or obligated. I feel I know what it's about, but I can't say it. Who cares anyway? There aren't many things I care about. It's just gonna happen."*

Kenneth A. Schmidt MS, LMFT

The new feminine part opened conversation that had never occurred between the masculine parts. They were too busy dealing with differences through unthinking combativeness to listen to each other. Can you sense Brian's desire for relationship with the girl? He never states it, but it's there. This becomes pivotal in future dreams.

I definitely would have had him discover and identify with the feelings of the building, but we ran out of time.

A few days later, Brian had a dream "experience" that was not a story. He became aware of a clear message. It felt like a realization and an answer to prayer. The message was: *"Just be honest. Don't fool yourself."* This seems to fit the role the girl played in dialogue. She called the men to honesty. Pay attention to these insights that come when you're dreaming or daydreaming. They often have meaning.

At his next session Brian reported, "I'm feeling less hostile now." His next dream is a shift from the previous two. The fight is gone, and another woman appears (characters underlined, the cab and the airport are not seen but only sensed so they are not characters.)

> *I'm standing outside an airport waiting for a cab. I got in a cab. The driver is a woman in her fifties. We drove off the airport property, and she says, "I'd like to show you something." I feel comfortable with this, so I say, "OK." We drive to an old house. We go in. The house is livable and furnished. It's not being lived in, but it is being kept up. I walked through it. There is some disorder, but it's not in shambles. I asked her, "Do you live here?" She responds, "I stay here once in a while." We get back in the cab and drive off."*

As Brian, these are the feelings reported in sequence:

waiting:	*OK*
in the cab:	*comfortable*

The Transforming Gift of Dreams

curious

calm

surprised at my calmness

in the house: *vigilant*

critical

surprised

evaluating house

OK

acceptable

nice

In identifying with this, Brian said that he felt this way in his growth. "I'm on the way home but still not quite there. I'm going to a better place, and though I'm not there yet, I don't feel alienated any longer." We then reached the end of our session.

When Brian returned three weeks later, he reported he was less hostile now and less critical of himself and others around him. We continued his work by staying with the same dream and having him be the woman in it.

WOMAN'S FEELINGS:

driving: *confident*

anticipating

in control

purposeful

calm

at the house: *comfortable*

allowing

unhurried

unconcerned

fitting

as expected

trusting

When Brian left the dream and identified with these feelings, he said, "Yes, I'm feeling confident in what I've been creating in the last two or three months." The woman revealed a confidence and sense of being "at home" in herself that was just beginning for him.

Feelings as the House:

shameful

unkempt

run-down

livable

easily fixed up

lots of potential

unhappy about my location—too close to airport

criticized

unwanted

when left: *abandoned*

let down

want to be lived in

Brian quickly identified these feelings as true for him. He didn't feel as good about himself as he wanted to, yet he was becoming more aware of what was possible. Having to travel and be away from the family too much (too close to the airport) bothered him, and he still wanted more life. Time limitations prevented our dialoguing this dream. Notice how the house has improved since the shack in the earlier dream. This reveals how Brian is growing in caring for his soul.

The Transforming Gift of Dreams

At the next session, Brian reported that anger with his children was no longer the issue it had been. He said he wanted to pursue self-expression more and become "who I really am." He shared this dream:

I'm watching my wife, Mary, and Johnny (a friend) outside the house in the sunlight. They are naked and engaging in foreplay. They became passionate, and I had the sense they were going to do this. I asked, "Are you really going to go ahead with this?" Then Johnny and my wife go off together.

This dream seems different at first, but it eventually reveals the same issues. He reported these feelings as the different characters in this dream. The house was not seen so it is not considered to be a character.

Brian's feelings: *afraid, anxious, alienated, angry, betrayed, aroused, cheated, jealous, disappointed, frustrated, left out, insecure, out of control, violated, resigned,* and *responsible.*
"When I spoke up, I felt disappointed that I had to step in. Somehow this meant I'd been defeated. I had hoped I wouldn't have to say anything."
Identification with Brian's feelings: *"Yes, I get violated and don't want to speak up. Eventually I get deeply hurt. I feel helpless to change it and even feel responsible for its happening."*

Johnny's feelings: My *opportunity* is here. This seems *consensual.* She wants it too. Apparently it's *OK* with Brian, and it's OK with Mary. I guess there's no reason to hold back. But then Brian speaks up, and I feel *stopped* and *confused.* I'm *asking* myself, "How did we ever get this far? How could we do this?"
Identification with Johnny's feelings: "Possibly feelings I have at times toward other women. A passionate part of me."

Mary's feelings: I feel *sensual, uninhibited, aware of Brian, ambivalent about the whole thing. No moral feelings, no anxiety. It all seems natural. When Brian speaks, I feel frustrated, guilty, and wondering, "How did we get this far? No one gets satisfied this way!"*

Identification with Mary's feelings: *"Yes, this fits my feelings about both marriage and financial success. I pursue both sex and money but feel ambivalent and without fulfillment, feeling frustrated and guilty and wondering why there's no satisfaction."*

Please notice that it was crucial that Brian not let any feelings of shame stop him from reporting this dream. As you'll see, it was an important part of his healing.

At our next session, this dialogue emerged from the dream:

Brian: *This doesn't seem right to me. I don't want to have to intercede or pull rank. Everybody's got to make their own decisions. I love you, Mary. I don't want to share you. I understand passion. How did it get this far?*

Mary: *It seems like it's all right with you. I could go either way. I'm ambivalent. It seems like it's all right. I can see why it's uncomfortable for you.*

Brian: *I don't want the decision to be coming from me. I'm jealous that you'd be passionate with another man. I feel angry and hurt. Is there something missing? Yet it's up to you.*

Mary: *I guess I've been assuming it's OK. Nothing missing. You've been passive. I was just going along with things. You've never demonstrated any jealousy. You're just not there emotionally with me. Intellectually?—Yes. But how do you feel? If you stay on that level, you won't meet my needs.*

Brian: *I know what I need to do. I have to go beyond the intellectual level and talk about feelings. I'll commit to that.*

Johnny: *What about going with what feels good? Spontaneity, passion, throwing caution to the wind. You don't know me. You've kept me out.*

The Transforming Gift of Dreams

You're wishing you could be like me. You've been passive. Why are you surprised?

Brian: *I would like to be more like you, but I want some respect for my relationship with Mary, and I want your friendship.*

Johnny: *You've got to acknowledge me! I'm a part of you!*

Brian: *I agree. If I'm committed to having you as a friend, I need to be committed to you. I need you in my life to shake me out of my passive routine. I just let things develop. Without you, I don't really take hold of life and enjoy it.*

Johnny: *I'm here. I've always been here. What we've got to do is work together.*

House: *Finally, you guys are getting your act together. I want to be cared for! I want you to live together in me and agree to work on taking care of me and helping me become more functional.*

Brian: *Wow. That's a lot to ask. I'm not sure we can do that. Mary, would you be open to that?*

Mary: *Yes, I would like that very much, and [to the house] I would even like decorating you.*

Brian: *We've just finally connected, and now we're being asked to live in the same house. Does this seem possible for you?*

Johnny: *I've wanted us to work together for a long time. I want this very much.*

Brian (to house, Mary and Johnny): *OK. It seems our answer to you is yes, we want to live within you.*

Brian and Johnny in this dialogue are the same two people who were fighting almost to death before. One of these parts (Johnny) is the passionate, life-loving, emotional part of Brian that has been demanding acknowledgment. The other part (Brian) is "responsible Brian" who doesn't say what he wants, allows others to violate him, and isn't able to love and be loved.

The female part has felt unloved and ambivalent about life. She's been going through the motions of marriage and life. This part could only feel sensuality. Brian's sexuality and passion (Johnny) were split off from the responsible, dutiful attorney, husband, and father. This is why his sexual feelings seemed out of control at times. They were alienated from the rest of him. This also led to his frustration with his children. Children are naturally life-loving and emotional. The responsible, serious, dutiful Brian couldn't stand that about them and lost his temper at their spontaneity. In this dream, they all came back together.

Remember these paragraphs of interpretation are to help your understanding because Brian didn't need them. The expression of feelings and the dialogue did the healing. If you feel frustrated that you don't understand all the symbols in this last dream, I understand. If analytical explanations were our goal, we could spend hours analyzing. We can't understand it all and do not need to.

Soon after this dream, Brian said he was ready to terminate therapy. He had achieved his goals and was ready to go on with life. His feelings had changed. He was more spontaneous, relaxed, and related to others more openly. He was not completely whole and without problems, but he was enjoying life in a new way.

CHAPTER 9

Boundaries: Establishing Who You Are

Boundaries define us. They define what is me and what is not me. A boundary shows me where I end and someone else begins, leading me to a sense of ownership.

—Drs. Henry Cloud and John Townsend

DAVE WAS UNDER tremendous stress. His business, his immediate family, and his extended family were in crisis, all at the same time. He was convinced that everything was falling apart. Yet just weeks before, things had been wonderful. His daughter was getting married, his family was coming to the wedding, and his business was booming.

But within the space of a few short weeks, the engagement was broken off, his daughter was heartbroken, his father became gravely ill, and the co-owner of his business died. His daughter was grief-stricken, the business and its employees were in chaos, and all of his family was upset. It seemed that everyone in his life was looking to Dave for strength and direction. Everybody needed something from him.

Dave's childhood survival technique was to take care of everyone's feelings so that they would like him. He was always strong, in control, and caring. He never noticed that he had trouble saying, "No" to people.

He'd always been strong enough to deal with whatever was thrown at him. But now, it was too much. He began to have anxiety attacks and feelings of hopelessness and depression. He came in to see me, and, in our second session, he shared this dream:

> The <u>house</u> <u>we</u>'re in has a roof that's leaking, letting in rain. The roof has big holes in it. If you reach up to touch the roof, material falls out, and a new hole is formed.

This is the dreamwork that followed:

> Feelings as Dave: *unsurprised, resigned, blaming others, this isn't my house, we need to get out, this isn't working.*
> Identification with Dave: "*Yes, my present situation feels just like this. This is how I feel. I know I've got to make a change. My way of living is no longer effective.*"

> Feelings as house: *Embarrassed, sad, ashamed, mad, disappointed, I'm not doing my job. I'm a failure. It hurts that I'm leaking and that I'm not already equipped to deal with this.*
> Identification with house: "*Yes! Exactly how I feel now. This sense of failure and discovering I'm inadequate to deal with what's happening cause me to feel embarrassed and ashamed about who I am.*"

Dialogue:

> Dave (to house): "*You're letting me down. You're not providing what you should! You're not protecting and shielding me. You're falling apart under pressure.*"
> House: "*You're right. I'm falling apart. My frame is sturdy, but my roof leaks. My frame is good. I need to be repaired and rebuilt. I know it's not*

pleasant, and I'm not providing what you need, but I've got a good founda-tion and structure. I need to be repaired."

Dave: *"I feel if I'm going to stay with you, we'll have to endure a season of rebuilding. We'll have to tear off the old roof and put on the new. I have to decide if you're worth it. Is your frame and foundation good enough for this? You might be, but I'm not sure."*

House: *"I understand that you're not sure because I've let you down. I know, and you know I'm worth it. My framework is strong and sturdy. We just need a new roof. I know you're disappointed, but all I can do is say, 'Here it is.'"*

Dave: *"I appreciate what you're saying and feeling, but I'm still unsure if I can trust you to be what I need you to be."*

At this point, the dialogue stalled, and I asked Dave if there was anything he wanted from the house.

Dave: *"Be patient with me. Give me time. I'm realizing I've got a lot going on. I need time to think before I make a commitment."*

House: *"I have no problem giving you time. You make the call. You let me know."*

Dave: *"OK."*

Afterward Dave said he knew the dialogue "should" end with the two (the house and Dave) working together, but he couldn't make it happen. If he had faked it, then he would have felt uncomfortable. Within himself, he would have known it wasn't resolved. Later on in this chapter, we'll see a dream Dave had two months later and compare this house to the later one.

The house revealed the state of Dave's soul. He wasn't protecting himself. His personal boundaries were inadequate. In other words, he couldn't say, "No," when he needed to. There was no "line" within Dave that clearly separated him from the needs of others. If they had a need, he felt compelled to fill it.

Other humans have not been given the authority to tell us who we should be or how we should think or feel. If they do, they are violating us. Parents have the authority to teach children the behaviors that will help them live. They can apply consequences so they'll learn what is best for them. But parents, too, are out of line if they try to *force* children to think or believe in a certain way rather than entrusting it to them. Human societies must develop rules and consequences to protect themselves from damaging behaviors, but that is not the same as evaluating the worth of a person.

Tragically, however, violation is often done in the name of God. Some religious people believe that God has given them the personal right to force their beliefs on others. If we decide how others should believe and try to force our perspective on them, then we are violating their territory and judging them.

Even if your intentions seem wonderful, imposing your point of view or behavior on another is a violation. If you decide someone should lose weight, for example, and try to change him or her by exerting power, you are violating that person. If you try to force someone to stop smoking, you are violating the person. The "good intentions" of the violator are irrelevant. If you are imposing your thinking or beliefs or actions on others, you are acting to destroy their souls, no matter what your intentions were.

Violation never accomplishes what we want anyway. Attempts to violate someone always end in frustration and loss. People who are being violated who can't say a direct, "No," will quietly resist and frustrate their violators. They may say they agree, yet they will internally resist, and nothing will change. Forcing people to do what is best for them is a sure way to ensure they won't do it! If they appear to do it, then they'll eventually sabotage the whole thing, leaving you frustrated. They may not be able to get back at you, but they will try to get even.

In my opinion, there is no greater sin than violation, and we've all been violated and are all violators. If you check the Ten Commandments, you will see that each of them is a law against a different kind of violation.

Most psychotherapy helps people deal with violations and learn not to violate. This is foundational. When Dave came in, he had no idea why he was anxious and depressed. This dream helped him realize that he wasn't adequately protecting himself because his boundaries were inadequate. People's expectations were overwhelming him because he couldn't say, "No."

But notice this: in his present situation, nobody was violating Dave; they just had intense needs they wanted filled. It was not present violation that was damaging him, but his absence of boundaries from childhood. If we have weak boundaries, the world is a scary place. Anyone who wants anything from us is a threat because we have no defense against their desire. We feel incredibly guilty if we say, "No," because we've been taught we were "bad" if we did so. So we must either withdraw or give in by trying to please. Adequate personal boundaries are necessary in order to separate us from the needs and wants of others.

The condition of dream houses or buildings often reveals the state of our boundaries. Someone who's been violated and is still allowing it may dream of a house or building with a missing wall. In Dave's case his "leaky" boundaries were symbolized by the roof of his dream house. As Dave began to say, "No," more effectively, he later dreamed of a new house with intact roof and walls.

As our boundaries become clearer, we know our true identities more accurately. Gradually, we more accurately recognize the times when we want to say, "Yes." This is why so many marriage partners, usually women, lose interest in sex in their marriage relationships. If they feel they are wrong to ever say, "No," to their partner's desires, their only defense is emotional withdrawal. They shut down emotionally and become unresponsive sexually. Only by saying, "No," sexually, will they ever be able to give a genuine yes and enjoy their sexual relationships.

As Dave's boundaries strengthened, he knew when to say, "No," and when to go ahead because he wanted to do something. As his boundaries developed, his stress level dropped considerably. Inadequate boundaries are probably the biggest single source of stress in most people's lives. Discovering when we were and are violated and preventing violations from occurring is crucial to our emotional and spiritual health and to our maturing. Healthy boundaries are necessary for healthy relationships.

Boundary development is usually easily traced in dreamwork. Before boundaries are healthy, individuals often have dreams of being chased or pursued, and their only defense is escape. This illustrates how we behave when we don't have boundaries. Our only defense is withdrawal. If we can't confront others who try to violate us, then we have to get distance between them and us. People with weak boundaries usually live in isolation. We need adequate boundaries to feel safe in relationships.

As people realize their lack of boundaries, they begin to develop them. Here is a dream of someone who is just beginning to realize that she has boundaries and is becoming capable of defending them:

I was in the shower. Someone entered the bathroom without knocking.

Here is her dreamwork:

Dreamer: I feel *upset, invaded, violated, irritated, annoyed, and exposed.*
Identification with dreamer: *"Yes, I frequently feel as if someone has stepped into my space without asking or treating me with respect."*

The Transforming Gift of Dreams

When people have never had boundaries, it sometimes requires months of work before they know they feel violated. In the beginning, they will use the emotions list, and, even in a situation of obvious violation, they'll go right by the word "violated" without hesitation. They're not aware of boundaries, so they can't be aware of being violated.

I will usually point out the word when they omit it and ask if they might feel violated. If they say, "No," then I'll ask if their logical mind sees that violation is occurring in the dream. Usually they then say, "Yes, but I don't feel it."

The dream we're considering illustrates a person reaching a "turning point" in dealing with boundary violation.

Notice the complete lack of boundary awareness in the person who is entering the shower area:

> Person entering bathroom: *aware of person showering, going about my business, no problems.*
> Identification with person entering shower: *"I guess so. There are no real feelings there."*

Dialogue:

> Dreamer: *"Hey, I'm in the shower. What's going on?"*
> Person entering: *"I'm just getting something I'll be out in a minute."*

At this point, my client said, "There's nothing more to say. I'm still bothered, but what else is there to do?"

I asked, "Is there anything you want that you might ask for?"

The response was, "Sure. I don't want them to just walk in on me whenever they want."

When I encouraged the dreamer to say what she wanted, she hesitated, and then replied, *"I would have never thought of actually saying it."* When she then tried to ask for what she wanted, she took a long while to speak. Finally, she said:

> Person in shower: *"I'd appreciate it if you would knock before entering when you hear the shower running. I'd like my privacy."*
> Person entering: *"Why? I'm not doing anything to you."*
> Person in shower (after another long hesitation): *"I just want my privacy when I'm showering. I don't want someone walking in on me."* There is an increasing sense of anger and personal power rising now.
> Person entering: *"I can't see why you're making such a big deal out of this. Can't I just finish what I'm doing?"*

Again she paused and said she felt stuck. She asked me why she was making such a big deal about it. I explained that it was important for her to say what she wanted, even if she could not explain why she wanted it—that it was all right for her to want space and privacy for herself.

I also reminded her that it was important for her to say, "No," when she needed to. This kind of permission-giving is often needed from the "helper" in dreamwork. Note the increasing level of intensity and anger as the dialogue continues. Anger has been given to us as a means of defending our boundaries.

> Person in shower: *"No! I want my privacy. There are some things that I get to keep to myself, and my time in the shower is one of these. Get out of here!"*
> Person entering: *"OK, OK. I'm out of here."*

At this point, she paused and said, *"That's strange. Somehow, as this person, it feels good to hear the other hold their ground. I wouldn't have expected that."*

I encouraged her to go on and actually say this in the dialogue.

Person entering: *"Thanks for telling me. I'm glad you did."*

This relief after a boundary is set occurs frequently. We know deep within that boundaries are good for us. When boundaries are identified and respected, it increases our sense of security, whether we are the violated one or the one doing the violating!

As people develop personal boundaries, they first become able to identify violation; then they feel angry when violated; finally, they confront and stop violation from occurring.

Boundaries Are Developed in Early Childhood

The absence of personal boundaries usually comes from damaging parenting during the second and third years of life. Erik Erikson identifies autonomy as the primary issue of this developmental stage. To develop autonomy is to develop an awareness of oneself as separate from others. It includes the exercise of personal power and the development of personal boundaries.

> *Children are egocentric because they have not had time to develop ego boundaries. An ego boundary is an internal strength by which a person guards her inner space.*
>
> *—John Bradshaw*

Without an ego boundary, a person has no sense of an independent self. The easiest way to understand this is that the person cannot say, "No," to another. When these people want to say no, they doubt that they have the right to do so. The healthy two-year-old learns to say, "No," "I want," and "Mine." In some religious homes, these words are anathema. The parents conclude that the child is insubordinate and perhaps evil and attack the child's attempts to use personal power with shame. "How dare you question my authority?" may be a parents' response if they don't understand child development.

To understand these children, we must move into their world. Two-year olds live in a world of immensely powerful and needed giants. Children at this age have absolutely no inkling that they could take over, as some parents believe they are trying to do. They are tiny beings in an overpowering adult world. All they want to establish is that "I am a person" in contrast to all the others out there, especially their parents. Before about eighteen months a child does not even realize that she is a separate individual.

A simple illustration may help. Imagine a little girl sitting and looking at a picture book. She sees a picture of a dog. She's holding the book so that it's facing her, and you cannot possibly see it. She points to the dog and says her equivalent of the word, "dog." She doesn't turn the book to show it to you. *She assumes you can see it because she can*!

She does not yet realize that you are separate persons. If she sees it, she assumes everybody does. The development of ego boundaries enables the child to know the difference between "I" and "you." If a parent feels threatened when people have different points of view on life, then this new behavior is disturbing.

Also fundamental to our independent existence is our ability to say, "I want." Again this is not selfishness, but a statement of independent existence. When children are robbed of this capability, then they are set up for all sorts of adult relationship difficulties. Their ongoing internal sense of shame and self-doubt about who they are prevents their true presence in relationships.

When you are doing your dialogue work, always try to check if the characters need to say, "No," "Mine," or "I want…"! As difficult as it may be for you to do it, there will be no resolution or reconciliation without it.

CHAPTER 10

Houses: Discovering Who You Are

*The privilege of a lifetime is to
become who you truly are.*

—C. G. Jung

BECAUSE OF THE importance of boundaries, houses are important dream symbols. A house consists of boundaries. The foundation, walls, and ceiling all protect the people within from harm. Since our boundaries define our sense of self, houses frequently occur as important symbols.

The condition of the house is important to note and work on. When people discover dream houses they claim as their own, it is often the first time they feel at home in their own souls. It is often a time of deep emotion and joy. Here's a dream from a man we'll call Will:

> My <u>wife</u> and <u>I</u> were looking for a <u>house</u>. We came upon one that I really liked, but I was afraid it was too expensive. I didn't want to even inquire about its price. She encouraged me to at least ask, however, so I did. When I asked, I was surprised to find it was affordable.

Feelings as Will: *"I'm feeling hopeful as we start looking. When I see the house, I'm excited but skeptical. It's too good to be true. I'm hesitant to check the price and surprised when I realize we can buy it."*

Identification with Will: *"Yes. Recently I've begun to believe in myself more and find myself feeling good. Then I notice it and get scared. I'm afraid to trust the positive feelings."*

Feelings as Wife: *"I like the house, and I really want it. I almost don't even care how much it costs. I want to try to get it, and I'm sure we will."* Identification with wife: *"I'm not sure. I very seldom feel that confident or assertive in going after what I want. I'd like to be like this."*

House: *"I feel neglected and unused. I'm in good condition, but I need painting and furnishings. I've been vacant a long time. All the curtains and draperies are pulled, and I'm dark inside. I hope Will and his wife will buy me and open me up to the light."*

I asked Will to check the condition of the house's foundation.
House: *"My foundation is solid and firm. It feels good."*
I encouraged him to check the walls.
House: *"Most of the walls seem adequate. It looks like one wall has recently been repaired. There are some interior walls I wish weren't there. They make things seem cramped inside."*
I asked about the roof.
House: *"My roof is fine. No problems there."*

Identification with House: *"I guess so. I think I'm a pretty solid sort of person, but I almost feel guilty saying that. It's like I'm not supposed to feel good about myself. It's certainly true that I've been neglecting myself for a long time, and that I need to start taking better care of myself."*

As I then encouraged him to consider that this house was his, his eyes glistened and he said, *"That would be great. I'm just not sure I can believe it yet or not."* Dreams like these are special experiences. His boundaries are functioning, and he begins to enjoy being the person he wants to be. In Will's case, he had worked through childhood violations before reaching this place. (This probably explains the repaired wall in the house.)

Saying, *"This house is mine,"* is significant. If the foundation, walls, and roof of the house are stable and strong, as Will's are, the dreamer's ability to hold boundaries in relationships is often good. If the person still has boundary difficulties, a wall will usually be missing or weak. If a person has never had a chance to truly be him- or herself, there will often be unexplored rooms and a lack of furniture or decorations.

A series of dreams may reveal a sequence of houses that gradually improve, becoming stronger and better cared for with each dream, symbolizing the dreamer's growth.

A person's dream sequence may start with an early dream with a house in the distance, then a house belonging to someone else, then a house the person is visiting, then a house for rent, and eventually a house for sale or a house that is his or hers. This reveals a gradual process of discovering that the dreamer gets to live in his or her own soul and make decisions about how to live. Without this awareness, a person can never truly develop a healthy personal relationship with anyone because he or she is still being dominated by others.

We can see this growth by looking at another of Dave's dreams two months after his "leaking roof" dream in the previous chapter. He began our session by stating that he had been conscious of his boundaries and appropriately using them during the week. Then he shared this dream:

> <u>Anne</u> [his wife] and <u>I</u> went to stay at the home of <u>Amy Grant</u> for five days. It was her personal home in Nashville. I talked to her on the phone while we were there, and she was nice, down-to-earth, and very friendly. The <u>house</u> was distinct, warm, and inviting. It felt good to be there."

Feelings as Dave: "*In her house, I feel familiar, comfortable, and at home. While talking to her on the phone I feel disbelief at how nice she* is, welcomed, and feeling awe and wonder at the situation. As I wander around the house looking at it, I feel at peace and at home."

Identification with Dave's feelings: "*I don't identify easily with this. I've never felt this way before. Nothing has ever fit me this perfectly. Yes, I'm starting to feel this way about life—just barely.*"

Feelings as Anne: *I feel the same peace, but I'm more surprised. I wasn't comfortable with coming to this house. I expected it to be different, but it's just what we need at just the right time.*"

Identification with Anne's feelings: "*Yes. I'm amazed at how comfortable I feel with myself lately.*"

Feelings as Amy Grant: "*I'm glad you're here. I feel welcoming and want you to treat it as if it's yours. I feel neutral and benevolent.*"

Identification with Amy Grant's feelings: "*Yes. This is a strong part of me. I enjoy being a host.*"

Feelings as the house: "*I'm an older house. I'm in incredible shape. I'm well-maintained, like new, solid, and experienced. I've seen and heard a lot. I have no leaks in my roof or windows [remember the earlier dream]. I have an incredible frame and solid doors. I'm beautifully maintained, not showy, but comfortable and humble. I'm naturally beautiful, simple, and open but I could protect the people inside if I needed to.*"

Identification with house's feelings: "*This is in me, but I've not yet owned it.*"

Dialogue:

Dave (to Amy): "*I want to let you know how wonderful it is to be here. It's wonderful and comfortable.*"

The Transforming Gift of Dreams

Amy: *"We're really glad you're here. I'm glad we had a chance to host you. Make yourself at home, and feel free to use anything."*

Dave: *"We will. We'd love to repay the favor."*

Anne (to Amy): *"Hi, Amy, this is Anne. I want you to know how much we appreciate your hospitality and how nice it is."*

Amy: *"When Gary and I bought this, we wanted to use it to make people feel at home."*

Anne: *"You've succeeded. We feel at home."*

Dave (to the house): *"It's great to meet you. You're the house of my dreams. You're completely open and at one with your surroundings. I feel incredible peace. You're at peace with yourself. You are the most beautiful home I've ever been in."*

House: *"I'm glad you can appreciate my simple beauty. Not everyone appreciates me for who I truly am. If they see me, they're not sure how to take it."*

Dave: *"I really recognize the beauty and humility of you. It's awesome. You are comfortable with who you are—not as compared to others. You are what you are—unique and just right."*

Anne (to the house): *"I have to admit, I didn't expect this. I had moderate expectations. It's not so much that you are the most beautiful house I've seen, but you possess a beautiful feeling when I'm in and around you. I've never felt this before."*

House—At this point, Dave said he couldn't speak what he was feeling. He said, *"The house knows 'I'm just being who God made me'—to speak it would demean it. The house feels holy. I seldom feel this way."*

I asked Dave (as the house) who his owner was at this point. He didn't even pause; he knew the answer immediately.

House: *God's the owner!* Then he exclaimed in wonder, *"It's me. Totally me!"*

In this case, Dave went right past the step of saying, "This house is mine," to his deep feelings of being at home and at peace resonating with his faith. Dave moved from having the leaky roof and inadequate boundaries in his earlier dream to enjoying healthy boundaries, joy, and peace in this one. In between, he'd worked through a number of other dreams that took him step by step to this place. Developing boundaries had helped him be at home in his soul.

A few people never dream of houses. For whatever reason, that symbol must not be meaningful for them. Remember these things were discovered by doing the identification and the dialogue, so it's best not to interpret dreams according to these discoveries. I share them to help you understand the symbolism and to help you ask insightful questions if you encounter houses in your dreams.

Sexual Dreams

Sexual experiences often occur in our dreams. It is crucial not to judge or accuse ourselves when this occurs, but to stay with the process. You may well discover that the essence of your sexuality is your desire for oneness with others. When a person reaches a place of new wholeness and unity, it is often symbolized by deep passionate lovemaking. It is experienced not as shallow, erotic sex but as deeply caring, affectionate, truly loving sexuality. This seems to be the ultimate symbol for reconciliation.

This makes sense if you consider the process I've revealed. If our goal is for the different dream parts to be reconciled, could there be a clearer symbol of oneness than affectionate lovemaking? Don't shy away from sexual images in your dreams. Sex is one of the fundamental characteristics of being human.

It is also perhaps the most damaged part of our humanity. Sexual dreams involving other people do not necessarily mean you want to have an affair. Follow the steps I've outlined, and work out the emerging issues in dialogue. If you decide you "shouldn't" be having a dream, you may be letting shame rob you of a beautiful experience that will strengthen your marriage, not damage it.

In sexual dreams, as in any others, however, be alert to boundaries. If you feel that what is happening is wrong because you're aware during the dream that one of you is married, pay attention to these feelings! There is a boundary being violated—the boundary that is needed to protect the marriage that's being hurt.

Work through the dream, including any feelings of guilt or wrongdoing, until you reach a point of resolution. If you can't do it in the first such dream, it will recur. Dreams that include these feelings of guilt about violating someone's marriage often have roots in childhood violations of some kind. They are important to work through.

To illustrate how dreamwork deals with the issues present when an adult was sexually violated as a child, let's look at a dream in the recovery work of a young woman I'll call Lucy. She reported a pattern of having affairs and not being able to enjoy sexual relationships. This was because her uncle molested her as a child. We had discussed this, but the power of her emotions did not emerge until this dream:

I'm in bed with a man. We're in conversation, in which we're saying, "No, we don't want to do this." We're concerned for his wife. I was having an affair. Then I was caught in the bed by this man's wife. I hid under the covers; then, while she's in the bathroom, I sneak out of the house. (The bed, covers, and bathroom were not visible in the dream.)

Feelings as Lucy: "When I'm in bed with him, I feel *ashamed, frustrated, irritated and angry with myself. When his wife comes in, I feel ashamed, deceptive, and guilty. I want to hide. As I sneak out, I feel relieved, afraid, lonely, guilty, and pursued.*"

Identification with Lucy's feelings: "*Yes, after I had an affair ten years ago, but also when I was molested by my uncle.*"

Feelings as Man: "*Throughout I feel OK; no one will find out. I feel desire and wanting sex.*"
Identification with man's feelings: "*Yes. While in the process of having sex, this is what I've often felt.*"

Feelings as Wife: "*I feel angry, surprised, betrayed, sad, disappointed, hurt, unloved, "and used.*"
Identification with Wife's feelings: "*Yes, in recent years with my husband.*"

Dialogue:

Lucy: "*I don't want to do this. I don't want to get in bed with you, but I fear you'll reject me if I don't. I don't want to be rejected.*"
Man: "*No, I won't reject you, but I just want you sexually. If you don't get in bed with me, we won't have the same relationship. I'll still be friends, but not emotionally. I might find somebody else that will.*"
Lucy: "*I don't want you to reject me, so I'll get in bed with you. But I don't want to get caught. I don't want anyone to know.*"
Wife (to husband): "*I can't believe you would do this! You didn't love me enough to be faithful. It was just sex you wanted. I'm surprised and hurt.*"
Man: "*I didn't mean to hurt you. I didn't want to.*"
Lucy: "*I want to leave. I feel guilty. This wasn't right. I feel guilty. I don't want to face you. I don't want to be caught. I didn't want to do this. I just wanted to be accepted. I didn't want a sexual relationship. I just didn't want you to reject me. I didn't want to hurt you.*"
Wife (to Lucy): "*It's not you I'm mad at. It's him. I can't believe he be-trayed and hurt me.*" To husband: "*We're married, and you hurt me. I feel used. You didn't respect me, and now you've used her also.*"

The Transforming Gift of Dreams

Lucy: "*I feel used too. I don't see how you could do this to two people. I shouldn't be here. I didn't stop you. I let you come over. I needed to draw a line.*"

Then a realization came. After discussion, she continued, "*I don't want to do this, but I know you're a dominant male, and I should be submissive to what you want me to do. That I'm...*" She paused as what she was saying sank in, and then she changed direction. "*This is silly! I'm not going to let you do that anymore! If you don't like it, go find someone else!*"

Man: "*I feel hurt. I feel surprised and defensive. I respect you for that. This is a good strength to have. I'm hurt and saddened, but I understand. I respect you for that.*"

Lucy: "*It feels good! I feel respected and proud. I was able to do it. It didn't hurt as bad as I thought. I feel strong and confident.*"

Wife: "*I'm still hurt that you would ever have that desire. But I see you accepting her saying no, and I respect your answer.*"

I interrupted and asked if she wanted anything from her husband. She continued, "*I want you to want me. But only if you want to. I want to know why you were wanting to be with her. I want the same respect you gave her. Just because I'm your wife doesn't mean I won't draw the same boundary. I want you to respect that.*"

Man: "*OK. I can do that. I want you to be honest with me, and I want you to be strong and to set those boundaries. I'll respect you for that.*"

Notice how identifying what each character wanted helped bring this dialogue to a point of resolution. This is usually how resolution is achieved: through an honest stating of what is wanted and an honest response to that request. This is not only true in dream dialogues, but also in all conflict resolution.

The dialogue revealed that a deeper issue had left Lucy vulnerable to molestation. She'd been raised in a family that emphasized male dominance. When a caring male approached her as a little girl for sex, she felt she had to obey. I have seen a number of women who were left vulnerable to sexual violation because of false concepts of submissiveness. Lucy had to realize she had the power to say, "No," and set up a personal boundary, even in the face of this male's "authority."

So often parents teach two-year olds it's wrong for them to say, "No," and then get upset with daughters who sexually give in to boys when dating. Remember, if your children can't say, "No," to you, then they won't be able to say "no" to others either. Children must develop personal boundaries in order to take healthy care of themselves.

In contrast, if a sexual dream communicates wholeness and internal reconciliation, there will be no awareness of someone being married or guilt feelings. It will be characterized by love, affection, and closeness. Just trust what emerges as you work on the dream.

These healing dreams of loving sexuality usually come after the dreamer has developed boundaries. They don't mean the dreamer's emotional life will now become "wonderful." When we begin healing and experiencing love, it often opens the door to realizing how much we've been hurt. Before the love experience, we had nothing to use for comparison. Now, after experiencing love through dream and dialogue, we compare our past experiences and begin to grieve.

In summary, be alert to boundaries and issues of violation as you do dreamwork. Always check if a dream symbol feels invaded, intruded upon, or violated. When you are able, confront the violation in the dialogue, and tell the violator to stop. When the issue first appears, you will probably not be able to do this. As subsequent dreams continue to bring up the issue, however, your strength and anger will begin to emerge, and you will eventually be able to stop the violation.

As part of your awareness of boundaries, be alert to the appearance of dream houses or buildings. Be sure to include both in your identification and dialogue steps. Note the building's condition by asking yourself, as the house, about your foundation, walls, and roof. If you decide to do repairs or additional construction on a dream house, go ahead and attempt it in imagery. If you can repair a damaged wall or roof in your mind, it will make a difference in your behavior. You will find yourself demonstrating clearer boundaries and having an increased awareness of violation. If you can't imagine the repairs, don't worry about it; you're just not ready.

Finally, don't assume sexual symbols or dreams are sinful. They are often wonderful symbols of healing and reconciliation. Sexuality is one of our most precious gifts. Dreamwork may help you recover your own lost sexuality.

CHAPTER 11

Helping Others

*I believe the greatest gift I can conceive
of having from anyone is to be seen by
them, heard by them, understood by them
and touched by them. The greatest gift
I can give is to see, hear, understand
and touch another person. When this is
done I feel contact has been made.*

—*VIRGINIA SATIR*

GERRI'S DREAM SEEMED simple, straightforward, and easy to understand. She had recently experienced a number of reversals in life, and some important people had moved away. We began therapy knowing she had much to grieve. In this early dream, she was standing in a social situation with friends, wearing a black dress and hat.

I quietly assured myself that we were about to face more grief. I asked her to discover the emotions she felt as herself in the dream. Her response caught me off guard. "I feel comfortable, alive, and really self-assured. Black is my favorite color. I'm wearing it and feeling really good about myself."

After adjusting internally, I told her how unexpected her response was! I was expecting feelings of sadness, grief, and mourning because she was wearing black. She stated emphatically that this was a positive situation. It felt good to be back among friends enjoying life again. I had assumed she was still grieving. Instead, she was emerging from grief and going on with life—wearing black!

Fortunately, in this case, I didn't attempt to impose my agenda by interpreting her dream. Unfortunately, at other times, I've encouraged people down some dead-end streets because I assumed I knew where they were going.

The first and most important thing in helping others with their dreams is giving up your own agenda. If we believe we know what they must accomplish, we will not only be of little help, we will also hamper their healing.

If you interpret or try to take them down your path, you will often meet with resistance, especially if you're right! I'll explain a few exceptions later. Never impose your perspective on another. You will be violating them if you do.

I must once again strongly emphasize here that you must not try to act as someone's therapist if you are not trained to do so. People are always giving one another advice and direction, but combining it with dream-work could imply to someone that you have professional training. Please avoid that perception by not adding your advice to the dreamwork.

For example, to those of you who might be tempted to use the Bible to "redirect" someone in pain, I suggest what Brennan Manning shares in his book, *The Way of Jesus*. *"When you encounter someone in grief or desolation, do not speak the biblical language known to you and available to you: stand with the wounded man or woman in his or her loneliness and brokenness, weep and mourn with them, and let your silence be your compassion."*

Dreamwork is mystery. You must enter into it vulnerably as dreamer or helper, not knowing the answers but prepared to listen. This not a time for giving advice or sharing personal beliefs.

I hope many of you decide to work through dreams together. This is a marvelous but incredibly vulnerable process. My first dreamwork groups have amazed me in that their strongest comments about their work emphasized their deep sense of community.

If you do this in love and respect for one another, it creates intimacy at the deepest level. Group members see and appreciate one another's pain and vulnerability, and judgment usually melts away quickly. Intimacy and community develop in sharing our pain. It's a special way of loving one another. As Scott Peck said in his book *People of the Lie*,

> **"Healing is a result of love. Wherever there is love there is healing."**

For a married couple to love in this way, you have to set aside your own relational pain to be present without prejudice for your partner. I make my living doing this, yet, if I do dreamwork with my partner, I must strongly "bracket" my feelings about what she's revealing and set them aside. If I later use something she's revealed to me against her, I destroy my ability to help. She can't trust her deepest feelings to me if I use them to hurt or analyze her.

A group of friends, rather than spouses, is best for dreamwork. For example, dreams often reveal sexual difficulties. If I'm working with my wife and she reveals sexual damage, I may turn on her because of my pain, saying, "I knew this was your fault all along." Good-bye intimacy and healing!

In contrast, if a friend reveals something deep, it's less likely that my problem has hurt him or her. I'm more able to maintain a neutral, yet loving, attitude. Notice I said it's less likely to trigger a friend's relationship pain. It still happens.

For example, if a friend discovers a part that reveals that he or she is too busy to attend to relationships, I may want to say, "Well, it's about time you saw that. You've ignored me for months now." This shifts the focus away from my friend's internal healing onto my pain and me.

The Transforming Gift of Dreams

The guilt and anger I stir up may paralyze my friend from working further. If this happens for you, let your friend know that you've lost your ability to stay neural and helpful. Encourage him or her to work further without you. At another time, you can talk through the revealed relationship difficulty. Very deep honesty, intimacy, and trust must be present to be this vulnerable with each other.

It's hard work to be with others as they do dreamwork. It requires intense concentration both on the dreamer and on what's happening within you as you participate. You must be *spiritually and emotionally present* to help. Making this an intellectual process will deeply disappoint you and will not help your friend. If you don't know what I'm talking about, don't try to help another until you've faced your own issues enough to understand. But if you find you're able to be there for another in this way, it may bring you the most joy you have ever known.

> *Helping another requires "radical empathy and emotional engagement through attunement, resonance, affect sharing, affirmation and self-disclosure."*
>
> —Diane Fosha

We can't help others if we believe we can "fix" them. We must know in our hearts that only love heals before we'll be of help. The way we can love them is set aside our own feelings to closely identify with the feelings they are experiencing as they work

It's OK if you want to take notes for them, but if this causes you to lose touch with them, forget the notes.

If you want to develop this depth of connection and understanding with a friend but you're uncertain of your ability to be emotionally and spiritually available, say so. Your confession of blindness may open your eyes to see. Agree that you may each occasionally try to lead the other down your own path. If this happens, confess it quickly. The other person will usually be able to distinguish between the path you're pushing them toward and their true direction.

Keep in mind—the biggest help you can give is in supporting and believing in someone. You can remain silent as that person works, and yet, through your presence, communicate compassion and a desire to understand. Never depreciate this. To know we're not alone in the midst of our pain or joy is a precious gift.

> *We cannot take this journey into our depths alone. We need support. Sharing our pain can unite us in loving community because we cannot handle our pain alone.*
>
> *—Gordon Cosby*

To avoid bringing your own agenda into play, follow the steps I've outlined precisely without inserting help along the way. Once you feel how the process works, you may intuitively sense something that seems true about your partner's situation.

For example, as your friend identifies the feelings of a dream character, you may sense anger. You may ask, "I wonder if you feel anger as that person. Does that fit for you?" Make your suggestion gently, so your friend is free to reject it. Spoken in this way, it can benefit your partner. *Do not explain why*; simply ask if the person has the feeling you are wondering about, and then trust the answer. Anything that causes someone to shift into thinking over feeling is a wrong turn!

I often sense something about clients' feelings and gently suggest it as a possibility. Often they say, "No, that isn't it." Often, however, they agree that the feeling is also true for them. I generally hold the feeling I'm sensing back quite a while before sharing it. I take time to feel the dream with them. Only if my internal sense continues and strengthens do I share it.

Once you have connected with what they are experiencing emotionally and you are really "with them," offering feelings that come up for you may help them discover a part of them that has been invisible. This can reveal something very new and valuable for them.

When I was in training as a therapist, I heard a story about perspective that I suspect is true, but I can't identify its source. I offer it as illustration rather than proof.

Some researchers did an experiment with newborn kittens. The pregnant mother cat approaching delivery lived in a comfortable room completely covered with vertical black-and-white stripes. If you were in that room, looking in every direction, you could only see vertical black-and-white stripes. The kittens were born into this world and stayed in it for weeks while they grew.

Then the researchers removed the kittens and placed them in a normally decorated room, with only one really comfortable piece of furniture, a sofa. A cat would love to sleep on such a sofa. They'd upholstered the sofa in vertical black-and-white stripes, however, just like the room they had been born and raised in. *The kittens never saw the sofa.* They moved about with no awareness of its presence. The black-and-white stripes were second nature to the cats, so they were not aware of the sofa.

When we grow up with certain rules of communication or ways of relating, they are all we know! Occasionally you may be able to point out the "black-and-white stripes" to others and open up possibilities that have been invisible to them all their life.

If we go directly from childhood families and cultures into marriage, we automatically assume everyone thinks and sees as we do.

It's healthy for us to assertively say what we want. People can't resolve their conflict until they say what they want and understand what the other wants. Marriage partners are often incapable of openly communicating their wants, but still expect their partners to fulfill them. If these wants go unspoken, there will be no resolution or reconciliation until each person knows it is crucial for the health of the relationship to honestly state them.

In the same way, it's often necessary for dream characters to ask for what they want to reach reconciliation in dialogue. I frequently encourage clients to do this. The client often responds with, "I can't do that. In our family, we were taught that it's wrong to openly say what you want."

If this person were to say, "I want you to love me," or "I want you to treat me with respect," he or she would feel selfish and guilty. As a result, that person never asks for what he or she wants. And guess what? That person has never experienced the resolution of a conflict through open communication. Why not? Without saying what you want, it cannot occur.

When I encourage people to break family rules and ask for what they want in dialogue, reconciliation eventually comes. This is often the crucial step that opens the door to change. But they would not have spoken these words without outside help. Why not? The words would have never occurred to them. They grew up in an environment where that behavior didn't exist. It was not a choice. Identifying these blind spots is an important way one person can help another in dreamwork dialogue.

To illustrate this, I'll share two more dreams. In each, I saw something obvious to include in dialogue that the dreamer didn't see. First, here's Tony's dream:

I'm with Tim [Taylor] and Al [Borland] from the TV show, Home Improvement. *Jill is somewhere. We go by a shop window with an old bicycle in it. It's an American Flyer, and it looks brand new.*

Al says, "That thing is ugly!" He doesn't know the bike is for him. We walk in, and Jill is there. Someone lets Al know the bike is for him. He gets emotional and says, "It's a beautiful thing!"

Feelings as Al: *"As I see the bike I feel sarcastic. It doesn't appeal to me; I wouldn't choose it. When I discover someone has prepared and renewed it for me, I feel loved, somebody made an effort for me, grateful, happy, and joyful."*

The Transforming Gift of Dreams

Identification with Al's feelings: *"I've always wanted someone to put effort into loving me. I feel like it's never happened."*

Feelings as Bicycle: *"I feel good, new, shiny, polished, and in good condition. When Al is saying, 'This thing is ugly,' I'm feeling not bothered at all. When I see Al is happy, I feel warm, accepted, and appreciated."*
Identification with the bicycle: Tony couldn't identify with the positive feelings of the bike at all. He wished he could feel this.

Trying to identify with the other three characters, the dreamer, Jill, and Tim, did not bring any clear responses, so we moved to dialogue between Al and the bicycle.
Dialogue:

Al: *"Saying this feels really awkward and uncomfortable, but...you're a beautiful thing. You're unique, one of a kind, with your own beauty."*
Looking back, it's easy to see that this was an extremely awkward dialogue for Tony, because the positive words in this dialogue never occurred in his family.
Bicycle: *"I agree. I feel good about myself. I know I'm unique. In knowing you appreciate my uniqueness, I feel confident and good about myself."*
Al: *"I agree with you. I'm glad you're mine. I want you, and I'm glad you've been given to me."*
Bicycle: *"I don't know what to say. I have a lot of emotions stirring but don't know what they are. I'm not even sure what it's like to be loved."*

At this point, as the dialogue was ending, I felt it wasn't complete. Can you see why I felt Tony wasn't through? If not, review the dream situation. Al received a beautifully restored bicycle. He likes it, and it likes him. What's the next logical step? I waited for Tony to see the possibility before him, but then I realized he couldn't see it. So I gently asked, "Would you like to ride it?"

Tony said he'd never thought of this. Then he continued.

Al (to the bike): *"I'd like us to go for a ride together."*

Speaking these words opened a floodgate of emotion. Tony had a memory flash that took him back to a painful rejection by his father. Sadness welled up, as he remembered conversing with Dad about this, and they had cried about it.

A boy from another family had constantly been with Tony and his dad whenever they did anything together. This other boy abused Tony and took his place in Dad's life. As Tony remembered, he said, *"I have never been alone with Dad. I've never had him for myself. My sister got attention, but I never did."* The simple words spoken in asking the bicycle to do something with him brought these memories back. He went through years of wishing his dad wanted to do something with just him. The pain brought up was part of his necessary grieving and healing.

Notice how difficult it is to accept that he's wanted in the continued dialogue:

Bicycle: *"OK. Let's try it. But I don't believe you really want to. You're just saying it."*
Al: *"I don't think I'm just saying it. I want to try."*
Bicycle: *"I'm willing to try, but I'm having a hard time believing it."*
Al: *"Here we go."* (He was now riding the bicycle in his imagination.)

Carry out actions that are suggested by your dialogue in your imagination, as Tony did in riding the bicycle. This can be an important healing part of the process.

The Transforming Gift of Dreams

This dream began a period of grieving that eventually led to an experience of "coming alive" after years of depression and withdrawal. Simply asking if he wanted to ride the bicycle opened the door to healing.

Dream situations occur for a purpose. They may suggest actions and responses that we're somehow aware of but forbidden to use. This dream gave us a bicycle and someone receiving it. Every child knows what happens next. You ride it! The dream handed us this. All we had to do was pick it up and go.

The second dream is from a young woman we'll call Linda:

Doug [her husband] and I are driving to a hospital to have our baby. We're trying to decide what name we should give it. I'm not pregnant.

We go into the hospital. A lady has had my baby—a boy. I'm disappointed, but the baby's healthy and OK, so I'm adjusting. A nurse is in the room, working.

My dad is sitting nearby, glassy-eyed, in a suit. I say to him, "Dad, let's go out to the family." As we get out, I start crying and blubbering on Dad. I'm crying hard—wailing. I go to Doug and ask, "Why didn't I have our baby?" Doug says, "Remember? The doctor did an examination and said you were too small to deliver, that it would hurt you. So we decided to have this lady have him instead."

Then I'm downstairs in the hospital getting a yogurt with my cousin Melanie.

We worked the dream through with dialogues between Doug and Linda, Linda and her dad, Linda and the nurse, and Linda and Melanie. I want to focus on just two aspects of the dream: the reactions and the resulting dialogue between Linda, the nurse, and the baby, and then Linda and her father. Babies and children are important dream symbols. The appearance of a baby in a dream often signals the beginning of new life for the dreamer. In this dream, we'll see it helped Linda work through an issue with her father. These were our steps:

Feelings as Linda: *"On the way to the hospital, I feel excited, urgent, and happy. Upon seeing the baby and finding out it's a boy, I feel disappointed, unsure, uncertain, foreign, but OK. As I saw my dad, I feel caring, questioning, and concerned. As we walked out together and I began to wail, I felt my dad touch me, and now I feel connected, safe, a sense of release, it feels good to let it out."*

Identification with Linda: "Yes. These are the feelings I had in meeting with my dad this week." (Note: the dream had come before the meeting with Dad.)

Feelings as Baby: *"I'm out! I feel cold. Things are unfamiliar. I want warmth and love."*

Identification with the baby: "Yes. This is the way I feel with my dad now."

Feelings as Nurse: *"Adoring, admiring but not too deep. It's just another baby."*

Identification with nurse: "Yes. I hate this part of me. I can be indifferent in situations that are very alive."

Feelings as Dad: *"Drained, touched by life. I saw my grandson born. It was beautiful, precious. I feel so lucky."*

Identification with Dad: "Not sure."

Here's the dialogue when Linda first sees the baby:

Linda: *"Oh my gosh. You're a boy. I'm a little concerned about how I can relate to you. You look healthy. I'm happy about that."*

The Transforming Gift of Dreams

Nurse: *"You're a cute, precious boy, a little baby boy. You'll be able to leave any minute. I wish you'd stop crying."*
Baby: *"I'm crying because you're not holding me. I want to be wrapped in a blanket and held close, and, instead, you're poking me."*
Nurse: *"Soon you'll be in safe arms. For now, you have to wait."*
Baby (to Linda): *"I'm a little scared you might not love me because of my sex. I'll accept your love."*

I had waited awhile, feeling a certain step was necessary. As time passed, I saw it wasn't occurring to Linda. It seemed so important that I decided to check it out. Have you sensed or wondered about what I was thinking? What is the first thing a young mother wants to do with her newborn?

Realizing this, I asked what the baby wanted from his mother. This is what followed:

Baby: *"I want you to wrap me in a blanket and hold me close and kiss me and love me. I want you to love me. I don't want my sex to alienate us."*
Linda: *"That was just my first reaction. It won't make a difference. I want to hold you and take you off that cold table."*
Baby: *"That sounds good. I'd like to be in your arms now. Love me, and hold me."*
Linda: *"You're perfect and precious just the way you are."*

At this point, Linda held the baby in her arms in her imagination. While doing this, she physically danced around my office holding him. I had not suggested this to her; it flowed naturally and unforgettably.

Baby: *"I feel warm and safe. I love it. She'll never let me go."*

Whenever possible, I encourage people to physically act out their feelings in dreamwork. Brain research reveals that the body and mind are not separate entities. The body carries our memories and feelings as much as the brain does. Whenever we include our bodies in our work, it helps us "know" the change we're experiencing. Linda's dancing around the room with her baby in her arms is an experience we won't forget.

It may help to know that Linda's dad had difficulty accepting her at birth because she was a girl. He expected a boy and wasn't sure how to relate to a daughter. Linda worked this through in the dialogue above, but took it further in the dream dialogue with Dad:

Dad: *"I'm feeling so touched. I'm also feeling sad for you and me. I'm sad I missed out on parts of your life. I wasn't emotionally there. I feel regret. I'm sorry that I wasn't there like I should have been. I want you to enjoy your baby and not hold back like I did. I'm sorry I wasn't the best parent I could be to you. I'm sorry."*

Linda: *"I'm so happy to hear you say these things. Now we can start being the persons we were meant to be. Now you can be for my baby what you wanted to be for me."*

Dad: *"Thank you for forgiving me. I want to be closer to my grandson and be there for you. I want us to share our love. I want us all present. I don't want you to make the same mistakes with your baby. I feel really happy now."*

This dream marked a major shift, not only in Linda but also in creating new communication with her father. He responded positively, and they're now building their relationship.

When change like this takes place in dreamwork, we can't count on real people responding as "they" did in dialogue. We may reach internal healing, but people "out there" may still be too afraid to relate honestly. If you decide to take steps toward reconciliation after working it through it in a dream, do so cautiously, remembering that in dreamwork, you are reconciling parts of yourself. If a character like Linda's father appears and you are reconciled, that may or may not occur with the actual person, even though it has been healed within you.

Regardless, after we've worked something through in dreamwork, we can deal with the actual person or similar people more effectively than before. Linda did this with her dad, and he surprised her with how much deeper they went than ever before.

I recommend these steps for helping someone with dreamwork:

1. *Only work with someone if you can be spiritually and emotionally present through the work. You must be able to feel as well as think accurately to help.*

2. *If you desire and it's OK with your partner, you might take notes. This can help.*

3. *Remind yourself that your role is to support that person in the process, not to impose your agenda or "fix" him or her.*

4. *While the other person is doing step one with each dream symbol, check your own emotional responses as you try to be that character. After giving time to discover the person's response, if you have a response that seems fitting, gently check it out. For example, if you sense a person or object is angry, ask, "I wonder if you're angry." Then let the dreamer's response determine if this fits. Your main tool in helping another is your ability to feel.*

5. *If you notice that a character or object from the dream has been neglected, point it out. If the person has no response, suggest starting with a physical description of the character.*

6. *If you know the person well and sense a way that he or she might identify with a set of feelings, suggest it gently. For example, assume a dreamer has described a frustrated desire for relationship. You know of frustration in the relationship with the person's mother. If he or she doesn't discover it, mention it, and ask if it fits. Always give the person time to discover it. If he or she says it doesn't fit, trust the answer, and let it go.*

7. *Of you notice an important feeling identified in step one has been omitted from dialogue, remind the person. Also, watch as the person works. If you see a change of expression or some other reaction that's not spoken, note the reaction, and mention it. Ask if something has been dismissed that needs to be remembered and communicated.*

8. *If, during dialogue, a particular communication stands out as obvious but never occurs, suggest it. Al Borland riding the bike and Linda holding her baby are examples.*

9. *When dialogue gets stuck, notice whether the characters have asked for what they want from each other. If not, ask what each part wants. Dialogues can frequently become long arguments without resolution. These are important times for each to figure out what he or she wants and to say it.*

If you help a friend in this way, you'll understand his or her soul in a way that no one else can. You'll discover you're alike in many ways. You may even discover things about yourself you've never realized. Doing this together breaks down walls of isolation and connects us with others in our depths. It's a special and unique happening, and I hope you experience it.

CHAPTER 12

Questions You May Want to Ask

The universe is not only stranger than we think, but stranger than we can think.

—NIELS BOHR, DANISH PHYSICIST

DURING MY SEMINARS, participants ask a lot of questions. Most of what I'm teaching is new to them, as it probably is to you. In this chapter, I'll share some of these questions and give brief answers for each.

Aren't some dreams just meaningless?

I have worked with over two thousand dreams now. Only two or three left me wondering about meaning. Clients often dismiss dreams as unimportant. If they mention this, I ask them to share them anyway; it's usually meaningful and important. Early in therapy, a client may find it difficult to connect with a dream, but when we look back later, we understand its feelings and purpose. Don't dismiss any dreams as meaningless.

Where do the symbols in our dreams come from? How are our dream symbols chosen?

The symbols are chosen by our subconscious minds to represent parts of us. They are selected from any part of our experience of life.

137

If a dream is about a TV show I watched the night before, should I still work on it?

Yes. Don't assume a dream is meaningless because you know where the symbols came from. If you saw a cowboy show and a character was aggressive and your mind needs to symbolize an aggressive part of you, it may choose that character through which to do it.

What does it mean if I dream about someone I know?

It means you've recognized some characteristic in that person that you also possess. That person appears in your dream to symbolize that part of you. For example, if someone seems rejecting of you, you may unconsciously select that person to represent a part of you that rejects yourself. The problem you are working through in the dream may or may not be a difficulty in your relationship with the actual person. The person doesn't necessarily possess the troublesome characteristic. It may be that you have "projected" it from within onto him or her.

A couple of times, clients in therapy had dreams about me rejecting or violating them. This doesn't mean I've done that; rather it points out their possible fear of that, or they are projecting it onto me.

Of course, if this happens, I've got to review our relationship and make sure it's not happening. If therapy goes well, later in recovery, they may dream of me, and I'll symbolize a part that is now caring for them. They have incorporated my caring into their souls. Remember this when you think your responses have no effect on people.

I always feel I've forgotten how the dream began. Is this important?

No. This is common. Almost everybody says this about their dreams.

The Transforming Gift of Dreams

If you have a lot of dreams and can't work on them all, which ones should you choose?

Choose the ones that seem most difficult because they bring feelings of fear or shame or issues that disturb you. These are important to face.

I've found interpreting my dreams to be helpful. Are you saying that intellectually interpreting dreams is wrong?

No. Intellectual interpretation is not wrong. Few of us are trained in it, however, and without extensive training, it could be wrong and even damaging. Trained therapists will never impose an interpretation on someone. To do so is to violate the person. I don't recommend interpreting because I don't believe it's your best option. The healing comes through the identifying feelings and dialoguing—and that comes from within the dreamer, not from an outside interpreter.

Intellectual interpretation often breaks things into pieces. It is a kind of reductionism. I liken it to peeling an onion. You can peel until nothing is left. We can analyze our behavior until all meaning is drained away. Why did I serve on that committee to feed the poor? Was it because I wanted recognition for myself or because I wanted to feel good about myself or because I hoped to meet new people? We can do this until all joy is taken out of life.

We probably do most things for mixed reasons, some positive and life-giving, some not. Analysis tears things down. The process I've shared builds up. When you're through, you have more than when you began. It helps you become whole.

Are you saying that, contrary to other dream books I've read, we can actually get rid of the shadow part of us, rather than just accept it as it is?

I wouldn't say you "get rid of it," exactly. It is even better than that—it is redeemed. It becomes a positive part of who you are. Since it no longer has to be in the dark, it no longer needs to be viewed as "shadow. The redeeming of the shadow part begins with accepting its existence and owning it as a part of us. In that way I can agree with these other methods. Once it's redeemed, that part of us no longer needs to be viewed as a separate, shadowy part of our souls.

Can evil appear in a dream? If it does, what should I do?

I have worked with two dreams in which, when the person became the character, it responded, "I am pure evil." One character was a dark figure in the background, and another was an enveloping fog. Amazingly, the two dreams occurred within one week of each other with two separate, unrelated clients. I said nothing to trigger them.

When this came up the second time, I was certainly surprised. It had never occurred in the fifteen years before and has not occurred again in the last twenty. Why? I have no idea. I'm just reporting what happened.

What is important is that, in both dreams, when we moved to dialogue, and the evil character was confronted with, "I know what you are," the character vanished. Both clients, without any knowledge of each other or any communication from me, had the exact same experience! Confronting evil caused it to disappear.

The disappearance of a character does occasionally happen in dialogue, but not often. To have it happen twice in the same week with two characters that said they were evil truly caught me off guard, and I cannot begin to explain it—nor will I try to reach any theological conclusions from it. I will leave that up to you and the spirit within you.

In my experience, every time someone has shared a dream image of someone who appears evil, that part has been redeemed by bringing it into the light. It is eventually revealed as a good and necessary part of the dreamer, but that is different from the two experiences I've mentioned.

> *What about nightmares? Are they different from other dreams? Should I be concerned if I have one?*

Nightmares are important and should not be quickly dismissed. They are usually an indication that something is "boiling over" emotionally. The nightmare is an important attempt to resolve a problem. The dream is a gift, not a curse.

Nightmares frequently occur when some painful trauma from the past is ready to be faced. Unless the dream overwhelms you with fear, it is best to use the same dreamwork process as with any dream. If a particular dream or series of dreams occurs along with deep depression, suicidal thoughts or feelings, or other self-destructive behavior, get professional help. We aren't intended to live our lives in self-sufficient isolation. I get therapeutic help when I need it, and I recommend it to you as well.

> *Why should I be concerned about what happened in my childhood? Isn't what I'm doing now what's important?*

I agree. I prefer to focus on the present-day issues in a person's life. For me, this is one of the greatest strengths of this dreamwork. We don't have to go searching through a person's past to discover what has affected him or her. The dreams reveal what is happening right now. All of us discover feelings or responses, however, which began in childhood and are damaging our present ability to live.

> *Should I try to own every symbol in my dream?*

If time and energy allow, it's best to check out every symbol. Quite often an easily dismissed symbol is the most important. It may be a significant talent or gift you've been given that has been painfully judged and repressed.

Of course, none of us has the time to do every symbol in every dream. Do what your time and schedule allow.

> *Why can't I tell when a dream figure is like my mother or father? I try to figure that out but can't. What do I do?*

I hope you recognize the problem revealed in this question. You don't have to try to figure out anything! This is trying to interpret and understand, rather than just experiencing the process. If you need to recognize a figure as your mother or father, it will happen. Don't try to make it happen. Just trust what emerges as you follow the steps.

> *A symbol for my mother has appeared in a dream. I don't want to be like her. What do I do?*

Many of us decided during our childhoods that we will never be like mother or father. Sadly, in doing this, we lose not only the negative things about them but their positive aspects as well.

For example, if your father was mentally ill and emotionally needy, you may have decided to never be like him because he brought so much pain. To avoid being like your father, you'd have to be strong and self-sufficient all the time. You'd always have to know what you're doing and why you're doing it. There would be no place for weakness or emotional difficulty. This childhood decision would force you to live without ever being vulnerable or dependent. You'd lose the chance to be loved.

Dreamwork often leads to "undoing" these childhood decisions. The dreamwork process will help you recover the needed parts that are like the person you disowned. But now they will be integrated with the other parts of you and not remain out of balance like they were with the disowned person.

Should you try to identify with just some of the feelings you discover in a character, or all of them?

You want to focus on the whole package of emotions represented by a symbol rather than just two or three. It's the set and sequence of emotions that the symbol is conveying to you that will move you forward. You won't make the necessary connections unless you consider the feelings as a group and in sequence.

When we reach this point in therapy, I read back the entire sequence of emotions for a character. Then I ask the dreamer to identify with the feelings as a whole. You may be unsure about one or two. Don't worry about every emotion fitting perfectly. You will probably sense it if your identification of a sequence of feelings is right.

In my dream, there is a character who affects everyone in the dream, but he or she doesn't actually appear. Do I include that character in dialogue?

There's nothing wrong with trying this, but people are seldom able to get anything from a figure that is "off screen." Apparently the figures we "see" are the only ones we are able to or need to consider.

Here is a dream that illustrates this:

I'm in my house. I'm walking with a woman (like my wife but different), and we're working out our differences. A guy is with us who's acting as a mediator. I don't want him there. The woman says she's been with him a year. There are a whole lot of people and dogs in the house. The dogs had totally destroyed a screen door in the house. I confront an older caretaking woman, asking, "Why'd you let them do this?" The woman responds, "I didn't let them do it; you did. I've seen it happening." I look at all the people and say, "I want you all out of here! This is my house."

Dogs had appeared in this person's earlier dreams. They had revealed deep fury at women. This fury was so strong that it seemed dangerous to the dreamer. When he owned the dogs in this dream, similar feelings came up. The dogs seemed evil, mean, and dangerous.

What happened during dialogue is what's interesting. As the dreamer worked through the feelings as himself and reached the point where he says, "I want you all out of here! This is my house!", he suddenly realized that the dogs disappeared at that moment—and a little boy appeared in the room. He'd either forgotten this when he shared the dream, or the change took place while he dialogued.

As we worked this through, we discovered that once he asserted his boundaries by expelling all the people who were violating him, the anger represented by the dogs was now expressed in a healthy way. Furthermore, his firmly putting up these boundaries made it safe for the child in him (the little boy) to be revealed.

In this case, the symbols actually changed as the work was done. The dogs were no longer necessary symbols, so they disappeared. The boy's appearance revealed a new part to be discovered and integrated. I share this now to emphasize that the only symbols you need work with are the ones that actually appear in the dream. Their appearance is not accidental or incidental. They each have a purpose.

Occasionally, a significant, usually strong, sound, touch, or smell in a dream have been discovered to be characters by asking the dreamers to discover the feelings that come up within them if they are the sound, touch, or feeling. If you try this and nothing comes up, just leave it as unimportant.

The Transforming Gift of Dreams

While sleeping, our vision and ability to move are both unavailable to us to use. However, we can still hear, touch, and smell even while we sleep so that we can protect ourselves. I suspect the absence of vision somehow relates to our seeing the significant characters as the ones who are important.

Do I really have to use chairs for the dialogue?

I strongly recommend it, although I know some avoid it because they don't want to exert the effort. But unless you are disabled or don't have a place to do it, use the chairs. Remember, we are physical beings as well as emotional and spiritual. If we were really talking to that other person, where would we be in the room? Where would they be? It helps us experience the differences between characters in dialogue.

When you become more experienced in doing the dialogue between different characters, you may no longer need the chairs.

When I dialogue, things seem to get muddled after a while. I begin to feel like I'm both people. What's happening?

When a dialogue is nearing resolution, people occasionally report this confusion. The two characters begin to seem so much alike, they can't tell who's who. This is usually good news, because it means you're owning both parts, and they are nearing reconciliation. This "muddling" emphasizes the need for using the chairs. The different locations prevent you from getting lost in the dialogue. (Note: reconciliation usually doesn't mean that the characters become alike; it means they agree on a resolution for their problem. Only in some dreams does this "muddling" occur.)

If I've identified the feelings for each character, do I still have to do the dialogue?

Yes, if you can. It is in dialogue that a lot of the healing occurs. If you can only do the first steps, they are valuable in and of themselves, and owning them will create change. But if you can take the time, the dialogue is usually an important step in the healing that might not take place otherwise.

Where in the dream should I start the dialogue if I can't decide? Is it good to just start at the beginning?

If no specific part of the dream draws you to it for dialogue, then start at the beginning. In many dreams, the beginning events cause all the events that come after. If the beginning issues are resolved, then the rest of the dream may no longer be needed. I suspect you will sense if this is so.

When I do the identification of feelings or the dialogue I often feel like I'm just making things up. Is this a problem?

You are making things up! That's what you're supposed to do. The point is that you can only make things up from what is already within you. This "making things up" reveals what issues are troubling you. As I stated earlier, this is why projective psychological testing such as the Rorschach test using inkblots and the thematic apperception test using pictures can assess a person's psychological issues. When people view the inkblots or the pictures and tell someone what they see, they are projecting their internal issues onto the blots or pictures. The things we see and the stories we tell reveal what is inside us.

Our dreams, of course, are even more accurate because not only do we "make up" the meanings as we do dreamwork, but we also made up the dreams themselves! If you are genuinely trying to "be" the symbol in the dream (rather than guessing at its meaning from the outside), and the thoughts or feelings are emerging spontaneously, trust what comes.

The Transforming Gift of Dreams

I started a dialogue by asking the other character why he or she was doing something. The character didn't know, and the dialogue could go no further. Something feels wrong about this, but I'm not sure what it is. Can you help?

Notice that "asking why" is asking the other character to think rather than feel. Usually this leads to a blank wall. Rather than asking why, express yourself as the character. Keep your focus on revealing who you are as a character rather than asking another to think.

When people deal with issues of abuse and rejection, they often want to begin with asking the abuser in the dream, "Why did you do this to me?" The abuser seldom has an answer—because he or she usually doesn't know why. Asking "why" implies that we believe we did something wrong that led to the abuse. It's often an attempt on our part to get control. If you eventually learn why the abuser did it, you'll likely find that it is because that person was abused and rejected too—and is compelled to repeat the abuse in an effort to understand what happened.

Why do I have dreams with a lot of characters? There's no way I can integrate all of them.

When people first enter therapy from a chaotic, dysfunctional background, their dreams are packed with characters. As they recover, their dreams become simpler. There are fewer characters, and the issues become clearer. When a dream has a lot of characters, it's best to choose the most significant ones, and deal with these.

I'm not saying that if your dream has a lot of characters that you are from a chaotic, dysfunctional background. There may be other reasons for the large cast in your dreams. It's also true that when someone's dreams shift from being simple and with few characters to more complex dreams with more characters, it often means that the person has begun to work on a new issue.

This has often happened with clients who have never faced or mentioned a molestation in their childhood. They'll be working and getting stronger, and then, probably when they now have the strength to face it, the molestation issues appear in a long, complex dream.

What does it mean when somebody dies or is dead in a dream?

Notice that we are thinking about this, so my answer will not always be true.

A person or animal that dies or is dead is usually a part of the dreamer that emotionally "died" in childhood. Occasionally people can remember exactly when this happened. Most of us, though, are not aware of when we "shut down" a part of our soul so we could survive.

The good news is that the appearance of the dead body in a dream is a signal that resurrection is about to occur. When this happens in your dreamwork, stay with it. Work it through. Other dreams are likely to follow that will continue the recovery.

I got all confused when I realized that a dialogue symbol represented my mother. Is the dialogue about her or about me?

Dreamwork dialogue is always about you. The part of you being revealed may have come from your mother or your father or other significant people. Often, as you dialogue, you'll feel it's just like a conversation you wish you could have with the real person. Maintain the perspective that this is something you are working through in your own soul. After you have worked this issue through within you, you may relate to the actual person in a new manner.

The Transforming Gift of Dreams

I tried dialoguing a dream, and none of the characters had anything to say. So I tried asking them for what I wanted—an action. A character was able to do it, and then a series of events occurred. Is this OK?

It's not only OK, I recommend it. Don't hesitate to ask your characters to engage in actions. If they can act in your imagery, it will create change. In my "wolf" dream, the lead rider holstered his rifle instead of shooting the wolf after realizing the wolf was no danger. When the wolf realized he was free to act, he grabbed the sleeping rider and tried to shake him out of his passiveness.

What do you do in dialogue if a part of you wants to take a particular action, tries to do it, and can't?

I've discovered that imagery is powerful in revealing what we're ready to change and what we're not. Let's say that in a dream you need to close a door to protect yourself from somebody who wants to violate you. In the dream, you tried to close the door, but could not. If I now ask you to close that door in your imagination, you won't be able to do it unless you're psychologically ready to do so. This may be hard to believe, but it is so.

I've checked this out with people many times now. It seems almost amazing. We tend to think that we can imagine ourselves doing anything. But we can't. If a particular action in imagery would be healing and protective for you but you aren't ready to do it, you can try all you want, but you won't be able to make it happen. Once you can imagine doing it, you'll be ready to move on to the next step of growth. Our imagination is an important part of who we are.

Is it OK to say, "I quit; I'm leaving," as a character in dialogue?

Contrary to what you've probably been taught, quitting is one of the healthiest things we human beings do. When we're growing up, it's necessary for us to try out many different activities and behaviors to see which ones fit our personality and abilities, and which don't. We're selecting from a lot of choices. Some of those choices simply don't fit us.

I've seen "little=league fathers" almost destroy their sons with their admonition, "Never say die. You can do it." Those of us watching this tragedy can see that the boy can't enjoy playing ball because it doesn't fit him. But Dad needs it to feel good about himself.

When a child gives something a legitimate try and discovers it just doesn't fit, it's best for him or her to quit and do something else. (On the other hand, if you know it's something your child genuinely wants to do and is capable of, then encourage persistence and determination.)

If you're from a dysfunctional family (which we all are to some degree), there are hundreds of things that would be good for you to quit. If you've been trying to get your abusive alcoholic father to love you and he never has, it's best to realize you can't change him. It's best to give up and say, "I wanted your love but never received it, so I quit. If you ever decide you want a relationship, let me know." This is often what wakes them up to what they're doing.

You may come across situations like this in your dream dialogue. Your decision to quit trying may be healthy. Keep in mind, however, that in dreamwork, the other person is a part of you. He or she won't disappear but will reappear in a new form in a later dream. The quitting will create change if it's a new behavior.

I've heard of something called "lucid dreaming." What's that?

Some people are able to change their dreams while they are dreaming. They can be active in their dreams, while most of us cannot. The closest

The Transforming Gift of Dreams

I've come to this is deciding to pinch myself to see if I was dreaming. I didn't feel a thing and realized I was asleep. It never occurred to me to try to direct the course of my dream. Lucid dreamers are able to do this. This is a new area of study you may want to pursue.

CHAPTER 13

Surprised by the Spiritual

Spiritual phenomena may be unconscious
or conscious; the spiritual basis of human
existence, however, is ultimately unconscious.
Thus the center of the human person in
his very depth is unconscious. In its origin,
the human spirit is unconscious spirit.

This is not unlike the eye—precisely at
the place of the origin, the retina has its
"blind spot" as the entrance of the optical
nerve is called in anatomy. In the same
way, the spirit is "blind" precisely where
it has its origin—precisely where no self-
observation, no mirroring of itself is possible;
where the spirit is "original" spirit, where
it is fully itself, precisely there it is also
unconscious of itself...That which does the
seeing cannot be seen; that which does the
hearing cannot be heard; and that which
does the thinking cannot be thought.

—VIKTOR FRANKL, THE UNCONSCIOUS GOD

The Transforming Gift of Dreams

I LIKE THIS quote from Frankl because it emphasizes the mystery of our spirituality. We cannot be sure such a thing even exists because it is not observable—just as we cannot see the blind spot in our eye that allows us to see. Paradox is part of the mystery and one of the reasons people give up on it as true is because they cannot use reason to discover it. It is beyond reason, so it often comes as a surprise when we're not expecting it. (For a great discussion of this, I recommend *Quantum Questions: Mystical Writings of the World's Greatest Physicists* by Ken Wilbur.)

As you will see in this chapter, the spiritual often occurs unexpectedly in people's dreams, especially in the groups I have led. Some of the dreams and quotes I share will include references to "God" and "Christ" because they are the names given by the dreamer. I will simply include these as they occurred.

These words from the "Big Book" of Alcoholics Anonymous describe my point of view on the spiritual very well:

> *Much to our relief, we discovered that we did not need to consider anyone else's conception of God. Our own conception, however inadequate [I would add that no conception of God is adequate!], was sufficient to make the approach and to effect a contact with a Higher Power, or God. As soon as we admitted the possible existence of a Creative Force, a Oneness in the Universe underlying the totality of things, we began to be possessed of a new sense of power and direction, provided we took other simple steps. We found that God does not remain aloof from those who seek God. To us, the Realm of Spirit is broad, roomy, all inclusive; never exclusive or forbidding to those who earnestly seek.*

My first "spiritual surprise" with dreamwork came from Steve, that very first client from chapter one who took hold of his dreamwork and grew unexpectedly. We did not see each other again until eleven years after our last day of therapy. My wife and I were led to change churches, and there, to my surprise, I found Steve and his wife Mardi. He had only mentioned church once when we'd been in therapy, and his comment was negative. We had never talked about anything spiritual at all. Now he was not only in church, but in leadership there. I wondered how that could have happened.

One day as we were walking into the Sunday service together, Steve said, "Ken, I have to tell you what happened after we stopped seeing each other." We didn't have the chance to talk then, but, a few weeks later, I went on a weekend retreat for which friends had written "love letters" to each other. We were to read these letters while we were there.

Steve was asked to write a letter to me. At the retreat, I sat on the floor and read his letter. I was utterly amazed by the "rest of the story" as Steve told it to me.

Dear Ken:

What a great chance to share with you the thoughts that I've wanted to write for a long time. When we met some eleven years ago, I had no idea where I was being led; in fact, the mere concept of being led was very foreign to me! Yet today I can see how God was using our visits.

When I look at that time and our work together, I see a personal emergence and transformation to a new person. You helped me to see by helping me lower my defenses and recognize my blindness. Your willingness to work with me on my dreams ultimately allowed me to meet my fears. It humbled me and led to my acceptance of Jesus Christ as my Lord and Savior.

About the time our visits ended, I was working on numerous dreams involving twisting mountainous roads with numerous obstacles and hazards. That series of dreams ended one night when I found myself suddenly driving to the edge of a broad flat plateau. A road crew was building a new flat, *straight, safe road. As I looked at the road I felt relief and joy and I heard the words, "Christ is the answer." Shortly thereafter I accepted Christ into my life and have not had a "winding roads" dream since!*

I truly believe that our time together prepared me to hear all that God wanted for me. It prepared me to be a new person recognizing my broken-ness and need for Jesus. I find myself studying the Bible and engaging in a struggle with others which keeps me moving towards God. Our time together started me in the direction of accepting God's will for my life. It's such a more joyous time.

What amazes me about our time together (~11 years ago) was that it involved dialogue between two men. In many ways it was a struggle with humanness that for me resulted in a connection and encounter with Jesus. Thanks for helping me with that struggle and helping me see that God cares and is involved with me.

Steve

Steve's words floored me. Our time together had changed both our lives. Steve's sentence, "I truly believe that our time together prepared me to hear all that God wanted for me," focused me in on the experience we had together as a crucial part of his transformation. Someone from a different spiritual tradition would have no doubt expressed it in terms of their tradition, but this was Steve's experience.

His letter reveals that Steve used our time to let go. He "lowered his defenses" and "recognized his blindness" and allowed himself to be humbled. This humility is crucial for our healing. Our choosing to be vulnerable and open somehow allows us to change. When I thanked Steve for the letter, we shared our amazement at how our time together had worked to change us both.

There were other clients through the years who had spiritual experiences during their dreamwork. Some of these people were Christians as

Steve became, but many were not. A few years ago, when I decided to start some groups in which I would teach laypeople this process, I had no thought of them as being "spiritual" or "Christian" groups.

As I shared earlier, one old friend phoned to tell me she was interested in the dreamwork, but, "I want you to know I am no longer a Christian." She had been hurt by the judgment of Christians and left the church. We had known each other in church previously, so she wanted to be sure about my purpose in doing the groups.

I assured her that these were not at all Christian groups but were solely for the purpose of sharing the dreamwork process I'd been using for many years. She decided to join us. Her question actually helped me clearly focus on the reality that these groups were open to everyone regardless of their belief system. We both had a surprise in store for us.

During our first few weeks of our group, I taught the process I've been sharing with you here. We used the dreams of the members of the group to reveal how it worked. We were having fun doing it together, and everybody was learning how to help one another as we learned.

Each person began to be able to identify with the other's feelings as they identified them in their dream. We all were excited about what was happening within and between us. Dave, a man in his eighties who'd been fighting cancer for years, was an active member of the group.

Early on, Dave took a big risk and told us about a dream he'd had, including some sexual feelings, which could have resulted in his being judged by people. He even said as he was sharing the dream, "Are you all OK with this?" The group assured him that they were right there with him, and he worked the dream through in just a couple of group meetings. We could sense that he was really grateful that he could be that honest with us.

Weeks later, he shared a dream that opened unexpected doors for us all. We identified a number of characters in it, but since it was very long,

The Transforming Gift of Dreams

we decided we couldn't do it all but chose one significant segment to work on. In this case, we asked Dave which part felt the most important to him, and he said the very end, which included a huge building. This is the portion he chose:

> The next scene is morning, and we are walking all over the town, looking at all the old buildings, some of which were empty, and others with a few people in them. Walking up a slight hill, I see a four-story building that is the length of a block. It was very impressive but also empty.

Even though he chose this segment, we still had to discover all the feelings of Dave, the dreamer through the entire dream. If we hadn't done this, his identification would have been incomplete because we must always identify with the entire sequence of feelings for any character. So we begin with Dave's feelings through the entire dream.

DAVE'S FEELINGS:

surprised	calm
amazed	relaxed
powerless	comfortable
helpless	neutral
change	startled
wondering	caught off guard
anxious	overwhelmed
questioning	disappointed
melancholy	puzzled
apprehensive	questioning
uncertain	disturbed
OK	a sense of waste

When I then read these back and asked if he could identify a part of him that has felt this sequence of feelings at some point in his life, he said that he had, but he could not give any particular time as to when he'd felt them.

The last few feelings in the long list are the ones that came up when he was walking up the hill and saw the huge building. He felt puzzled, questioning, disturbed, and a sense of waste because this beautiful building was not being used.

As that *huge building* just over the hill, he discovered these feelings within:

> *powerful*
>
> *imposing*
>
> *large*
>
> *bright*
>
> *strong*
>
> *attractive*
>
> *just there—I just am*

When I asked about his foundation, as we do with all houses or buildings, he quickly said, *"My foundation is solid and strong."*

When asked if he could identify a part of himself that felt these feelings, he replied that he could not really identify with a part like this, although it felt great.

We prepared for dialogue, with Dave deciding that the character "Dave" would be in the chair he was already sitting in next to me. He then placed the other characters that he said were present in this segment in chairs and a sofa around us in the room.

After a long hesitation, he placed the huge building behind the sofa, directly ahead of us. (The hill was in the sofa, so he placed the building behind it, as it had been in the dream.) We had to place a chair behind the sofa for this character, because no one in the group had ever placed a character there before.

Dave's dialogue focused on the other characters for a while, and then he shifted to addressing the building, and then changed chairs to be the building as they dialogued.

> Dave (to the building): *"How big and solid you are. What are you doing here? You're out of place."*
> Building: *"I'm here. I'm bigger than you are. I am here."*
> Dave: *"Why are you here? You're out of place. You don't fit in with the rest of the town."*
> Building: *"I'm still here regardless."*
> Dave: *"I have to accept that. There's nothing I can do. I am disgusted. It's ludicrous—but nothing I can do. Here you are—you are a waste."*

The next time Dave moved to the chair behind the sofa to be the building, something unexpected happened. When I again recited his feelings as the building back to him, he suddenly responded as the building, *"Oh my! This is God!"*

We were all caught off guard by this response, and I asked what he meant by that. He replied that he had just realized as he sat down in this chair that the character represented God. As I looked back at the building's feelings: *powerful, imposing, large, bright, strong, attractive, just there—"I just am"—with a solid and strong foundation,* I realized these feelings could represent God, although I had never experienced anyone saying this before in all the years I'd done dreamwork.

Then as the building, Dave said, *"I want you to come and live in me."*

After returning to his own chair, Dave responded by looking uncomfortable and saying, *"I'm not sure I want to do this."*

I encouraged Dave by saying something like, *"But Dave, you know that God wants all of us to come to him."* In the back of my mind, but not spoken, I was wondering if Dave was thinking what I suspected he was, that he was being invited to be with God by dying.

After a long, reflective pause, Dave decided to go and live in that beautiful building. He stood up and walked over to the chair this character was in and sat in the chair with the building. He had accepted the invitation and was now in the building.

I will never forget his face as I looked across the room at him sitting behind the sofa. With a relaxed smile on his face, he said, *"I feel at peace."* All of us in the group were taken aback and caught off guard, but Dave was feeling at peace as he sat "in the building" that had invited him in. We thanked Dave for sharing all of this with us and were wondering what this might mean for him.

Dave was sick the following week, so he didn't come to the group. But as if to emphasize the deep meaning of what we'd experienced with him, some other surprising events followed. That next week, a person who had not been there when Dave worked through his dream of the building volunteered to work on hers.

When we got to the dialogue portion of her work, she placed a character in the very same place that Dave had placed his character that "became God." The rest of us were surprised at this but kept quiet as she continued her work.

After a little while, as she worked on her dialogue, she said that the character in that chair felt "spiritual" to her, and, as before, the feelings from that chair were easily seen as depicting what Dave had called "God."

We commented on this only after she finished her dialogue—but everybody was amazed that the same chair was placed in this unusual place, and then represented the spiritual part of a person!

As if this weren't strange enough, the next person who worked through a dream and who also had not been present during either of the previous two—again, with no prompting, placed a person in dialogue behind that sofa in the same place and, once again, it was found to be a spiritual part of the dreamer. We had no explanation and were all wondering what was going on.

While this was happening, Dave had not returned to the group because he was still sick. Then I heard he was doing poorly and was in the hospital, so I went to visit him. As I walked in his room, he was sitting on his bed. He looked up at me and said with simple certainty, "This is it, Ken." Then he focused and said, "I am at peace."

We both knew that he was repeating what he'd discovered from his dream. The peace he'd received in his dream was a welcoming message to him as he began his time of death. He died a couple of weeks later, and our group could barely believe what had happened with Dave and his dream.

> *The inward stirring and touching of God makes us hungry and yearning; for the Spirit of God hunts our spirit; and the more it touches it, the greater our hunger and our craving.*
> *And this is the life of love in its highest working, above reason and above understanding; for reason can here neither give nor take away from love, for our love is touched by Divine Love.*
> —*John of Ruysbroeck*

I will share one other of the many dreams our group experienced to emphasize how the spiritual revealed itself unexpectedly. Mia is a woman who had also hesitated to join the group because of the pain she had experienced through some church experiences. This dream is one that helped her rediscover her spiritual self without anybody evaluating it. John is her husband, and here is her dream:

> *John and I are in a bathroom, having locked the door. We are crouching in the bathtub. People are trying to get inside the bathroom to hurt us. They begin shooting at the door.*

When the firing ceases, we get up to check...and find that there is only a <u>small hole</u> in the door. The shooting resumes, and we again crouch in the tub. I wonder at the strength of the door—it's only made of wood, yet it is still standing in all that gunfire!

The objects and people Mia saw in her dream—the characters—are underlined. As usual, we first discover the feelings of a character, and then see if we can identify with that sequence of feelings as part of our life.

Feelings as Mia: *extremely fearful, anxious, heart-racing, tentative, relaxing, then fearful again, somewhat protected yet vulnerable, surprised and impressed (at door still being intact)*

Identification with Mia's feelings: *"Yes, this is my way of dealing with problems."*

Feelings as John: *passive, just there, nothing to add, shadowy*
Identification with John's feelings: *"During my first marriage and with my Dad as his young daughter."*

Feelings as the Bathroom: *solid, dark, cold, lonely, but safe, secure, protected*
Identification with Bathroom's feelings: *"When I was a child."*

Feelings as the door: *solid, impenetrable, undefeatable, unexplainable, mysterious, protecting, surprising*

Identification with the door's feelings: *"How I feel about God."*

Feelings as the bathtub: *safe, solid, secure, protecting, loving, giving*
Identification with Bathtub's feelings: *"What I feel as a mother."*

The Transforming Gift of Dreams

Feelings as the bullet hole: *small, tired, exhausted, light, airy, free, finally successful, letting in light*

Identification with Bullet Hole's feelings: *"What I felt as I was leaving my marriage*

Here is the dialogue:

Mia: *"Hey John, I'm worried. I need help with this—how do we protect ourselves?"*
John: *"I'm here—support you all the way. What would you like me to do?"*
Mia: *"Talk to me so we can work this out. Tell me what you want me to do."*
John: *"I can give you ideas—talk to people outside."*
Mia: *"We are protected inside this protected area—no way a bullet will get through. We can wait it out."*
John: *"Sounds like a great idea."*
Tub: *"You are safe. I will protect you. I'm not cracked; I'm strong. You'll be OK. I don't know how long we'll have to wait. Do you agree, Bathroom?"*
Bathroom: *"You are safe and protected, but I'm not the best place. I feel dark and cold and lonely. It feels good to have you in me. I'm alone a lot. Now I have people to get closer to. I'd like to be loved, but you you've made it better. I feel completely protected. The door is withstanding the onslaught."*
Tub: *"We're kind of the same. We've been together for years and years and years. We'll continue in this way. I'm glad for you two friends inside of me."*
Mia: *"But they're trying to get in; I'm afraid."*
Door: *"I am the door, and nothing can get through. I know what's going on outside and in here. You can rest assured. Some of those bullets will get through. It's OK that you're surprised, but you are in good hands."*
Mia had tears as she said this.

Hole: "*Even though I come from a bullet—very scary!—I have allowed you two to experience pain and light. It's a paradox. The bullet hole provided the light. What you are most afraid of won't overcome you.*"

Door: "*I like you, Hole, because you let the light in. Hole, this is about letting Mia, John, and the Bathroom experience fear, and yet know that I am here. They may think that I'm wooden and can be broken through. You've gotten through a little, but not enough to harm them.*"

Mia: "*Well, I'm so surprised, Door, that once again you've proved me wrong by protecting me. I still feel, John, that you have been paralyzed in this. Can you say something to let me know you have a voice in this?*"

John: "*I've just been listening.*"

Mia: "*Well, that doesn't help.*"

John: "*I don't have the same worries as you. I don't need to be part of your drama. I can be secure with you and be with you. Don't worry about me.*"

Mia: "*Yeah, I agree with you.*"

Bathroom: "*I watch you all with joy and laughter. I feel more stoic, but it's OK. I'm just a part of you.*"

Mia "slipped" out of dialogue in that last line as she realized that the stoic feeling was just "a part of her," but that happens at times, especially when you are feeling the wholeness and peace that comes when a complete reconciliation has occurred.

Her dialogue reveals a very deep spiritual reality that many people have written about, including Father Richard Rohr:

The heart is normally opened through a necessary hole in the soul, a sacred wound. Our wound is the only way, it seems, for us to get out of ourselves and for grace to get in.

If you find it hard to believe the connections that occurred in the group's dreamwork with the perspectives of spiritual authors, so did we. This includes the idea that our suffering is paradoxically the very thing that enables us to experience joy and allows the light of the spirit to enter into us. So not only is the spiritual revealed here, but also a perspective on it that has taken theologians and mystics years to discover.

Teri, one of the group members, described in a letter her perspective on the surprising spiritual experiences we had unexpectedly shared:

Ken,

The beauty of the dreamwork for me is that I've been led through my dreams to explore the spiritual side of myself—the God in Me (without someone prefacing this experience as being good or having anything to do with being Christians, seculars and/or atheists. The idea of that would make me run for the hills!)

The way it happens in the dreamwork for me is intrinsic, so to speak, and it is so meaningful, meeting me exactly on the level or where at the moment I need to be met. This is a spiritual experience for me.

I'm truly just speaking for myself. It is church for me. Probably because it's the dreamwork that adds the spiritual component, not people who like us to think that their church or belief system or lack of it is correct or necessary. And it's not necessary either to have a religious system in place. Actually anyone can do it. That's the beauty of it. We are internally hard-wired to have that spiritual part—whether or not we see it in our dreams or not. Eventually all roads lead to Rome…or not.

So when I "do a dream" with a family member or friend I never bring up any churchy aspect of it at all because it truly is what it is—for that person. It wouldn't be fair to put my judgment of what that character symbolizes for that person. And if they discover a God-part of them, so be it. It is what it is.

There have been times in my dreamwork where I felt helped to see that part and I went with it, not truly seeing it, but perhaps others around me grew excited for me to see that part. The longer I do it, my boundaries *become better and I can negate which emotions that are not the ones I own. I'm happy for that and am glad to be becoming more true to myself day by day.*

This is what gets me excited to share the dreamwork with people. These are the things that will draw people to it...to learn and grow from their dreams.

Teri

I want to emphasize one sentence from Teri's letter—"*I'm truly just speaking for myself. It is church for me.*" Why was our dream group "church" for Teri, who had given up going to church years before?

One day, as we were finishing our time together, one member of the group said, "We don't want to leave!" As we discussed the feeling we were all experiencing that day, we concluded that we had become community in just a few weeks together. We realized, as a group, that the reason was that we had all been deeply honest with one another to the point of revealing some of our deep brokenness and imperfection, and then, when we did this, we discovered everybody was not only OK with it, but were truly there with us and for us.

All of us, without even realizing it, were giving one another grace— an unconditional acceptance and caring that we had received nowhere else. This is why Teri describes her experience as being "church." It's because this kind of connection is what church or community is supposed to be all about.

You need not be in community to do this work, however. If you are willing to allow yourself to feel feelings you've avoided and honestly discover parts of you that you really won't like as well as other parts that reveal a depth and power you never imagined, then you can do it without another leading you. This is a way of recovering your awareness of real life, which was taken from you by a world that judged who and how you should be.

The Transforming Gift of Dreams

I'm not saying that you will necessarily discover or experience the spiritual in your own dreamwork. Not everybody does. I'm only communicating my experience with this process, which I know changes lives.

We'll end here, and I want to wish you the best of life. I hope that what I've passed on to you in these pages will bring you healing, new life, and a sense of peace whoever you are and wherever you are in life.

Namaste, I honor the divine in you.

Recommended Reading (* for those most used for this book)

The Accidental Mind by David J. Linden

The Biology of Transcendence: A Blueprint of the Human Spirit by Joseph Chilton Pearce

The Body Never Lies: The Lingering Effects of Cruel Parenting by Alice Miller

Breathing Under Water: Spirituality and the Twelve Steps by Richard Rohr

The Developing Mind: How Relationships and the Brain Interact to Shape Who We Are by Daniel J. Siegel

*Fingerprints of God: What Science Is Learning About the Brain and Spiritual Experience:*by Barbara Bradley Hagerty

Gestalt Therapy: Excitement and Growth in the Human Personality by Frederick S. Perls

God is Not Dead: What Quantum Physics Tells Us about Our Origins and How We Should Live by Amit Goswami

The Healing Power of Emotion: Affective Neuroscience, Development and Clinical Practice by Daniel J. Siegel; Marion Solomon; Diana Fosha

How God Changes Your Brain: Breakthrough Findings from a Leading Neuroscientist by Andrew Newberg M.D.

Integral Spirituality: A Startling New Role for Religion in the Modern and Postmodern World by Ken Wilber

It Didn't Start with You: How Inherited Family Trauma Shapes Who We Are and How to End the Cycle by Mark Wolynn

Kenneth A. Schmidt MS, LMFT

A Little Book on the Human Shadow by Robert Bly

*The Mindful Brain: Reflection and Attunement in the Cultivation of Well-Being by Daniel J. Siegel

*Mindsight: The New Science of Personal Transformation by Daniel J. Siegel

Ten Thousand Dreams Interpreted, or what's in a dream: a scientific and practical exposition by Gustavus Hindman Miller

*The Transforming Power of Affect: A Model for Accelerated Change by Diana Fosha

*The Mind-Brain Relationship by Regina Pally

Boundaries: When to Say YES When to Say NO To TakeControl of Your Life by Dr. Henry Cloud and Dr. John Townsend

Appendix: Feeling Words

Discover all the feelings that come up within or stand out for you.
Do not limit yourself to this list.

angry
annoyed
irritated
furious
outraged
resentful
hateful
attacking
rejecting
critical

disgusted
fed up
repulsed
offended

jealous
envious

possessive
vengeful

dominating
controlling
violating
superior

rebellious
resistant
stubborn
rigid

distrustful
doubtful
suspicious
skeptical
pessimistic

unhappy
miserable
complaining

uncaring
indifferent
ambivalent
apathetic
cold

false
deceptive

hurt
abused
betrayed
deprived

frustrated
let down
hindered
blocked

manipulated
used
mistreated

deceived
tricked
cheated

dominated
controlled
threatened
intimidated
manipulated
bullied
smothered

attacked
judged
blamed
invaded
violated
belittled
persecuted
degraded
insulted

obligated
required
no choice

trying
striving
burdened
overloaded
overworked

The Transforming Gift of Dreams

neglected
abandoned
rejected
excluded
alienated
left out
invisible

afraid
concerned
anxious
stressed
defensive
worried
frightened
frantic
panicky
hysterical

alone
lonely
avoided
ignored
forgotten
forsaken

ashamed
embarrassed

guilty
at fault
responsible
remorseful

humiliated
disgraced
exposed
degraded
ridiculed
disrespected
squelched

depressed
hopeless
unmotivated
powerless
helpless
empty
giving in
giving up
despair
dread

withdrawn
detached
shut down
inhibited

passive
bottled up
numb

destroyed
fragmented
devastated
doomed

loss
grieving
mournful
gloomy

tired
exhausted
drained
resigned
defeated

failure
defeated
falling short

confused
disorganized
chaotic
hectic
messy
muddled
frenzied

inadequate
incompetent
incapable
unprepared
worthless

vulnerable
weak
insecure
small
dependent
needy

cautious
thoughtful
uncertain
hesitant
guarded
torn

broken
damaged
shattered

questioning
inquiring
curious

The Transforming Gift of Dreams

puzzled
wondering
deliberating

surprised
shocked
startled
amazed
in awe

wanting
desiring
pleading

hopeful
optimistic
expectant

accepted
forgiven
affirmed
respected
valued
heard

safe
relieved
secure
protected

loved
cared for
nurtured
desired
special

accepting
letting go

grateful
appreciative

capable
strong
competent
powerful

confident
determined
persistent

responsible
cooperative
valued

realistic
alert
lucid
sensible
logical

peaceful
calm
relaxed
contented

purposeful
inspired
clear-headed

loving
caring
giving
accepting
appreciative
empathetic
sympathetic

intimate
close
warm
affectionate
trusting

focused
motivated
engaged

complete
whole
fulfilled
satisfied
alive
vibrant

joyful
ecstatic
exuberant
renewed
energized
free
playful
childlike

Acknowledgments

MANY PEOPLE HAVE made this book possible, so I want to recognize a number of them. The first person who comes to mind is my personal editor, Mary Davis, who has worked with me for years and has always helped me find a better way of saying things as well as correcting my grammar.

Then come the people who have been part of the dreams groups that I have had at my house for three years now. They have all helped me see what laypeople could accomplish by coming together and honestly and vulnerably revealing themselves to one another. Through these groups, I discovered far more than I had ever known by just using this with people one-on-one. Your development of genuine community caught me off guard and gave me greater impetus to write this book.

I also want to express my appreciation to all the clients who trusted me with their lives through thirty years of using this process. Your work revealed so much of what I learned and shared here. I especially thank those who permitted me to use their dreams.

I am grateful to Steve Treanor who helped me discover the power of this process by taking it more seriously than I did back in the 1980s. It's been a blessing to be good friends for over twenty-two years now.

Kenneth A. Schmidt MS, LMFT

Barbara, my wife of forty-three years, supported me throughout those years, until she died in 2008. This would have been impossible without her support.

I also want to specifically thank Tania Sussman, Teri Smith, Linnea Taylor and Michael Johnston for reading over my writings as I tried to find the right audience and the right words. Also thank you to my new partner, Jeanie Ball, for supporting and helping me in recent years.

To you all, no matter what your contribution, you are an integral part of the healing and new life that these words will bring to people. Thank you!

About the Author

KEN SCHMIDT WAS raised in a rural section of Fresno, California, and graduated from California State University at Fresno in 1964. His college major was physics, and he worked as a physics and math teacher for seventeen years at Buena High School in Ventura, California. In 1972, he earned a master's degree in science teaching from Wisconsin State University at Superior where he learned a new way of approaching the teaching of physics, developed at Harvard University.

He was happily married to Barbara for forty-three years until her death in 2008. Ken is proud of the productive lives their three children Diane, Mark, and Karen are living, and he has been blessed with five grandchildren, Katie, Connor, Amber, Brennan, and Dorothy.

In 1978, Ken was led to change careers to become a psychotherapist. He earned a master's degree from California Lutheran College and was licensed as a marriage and family therapist in 1981. He had a successful private practice for thirty-five years, focusing on individual therapy because of his adaptation of gestalt dreamwork shared in this book. He has written two previous books, *Finding Your Way Home* in 1979 and *Promised Joy* in 2012, both of which are still available at Amazon.

In 1992, Ken contracted acute leukemia and was expected to die. He chose to undergo an experimental stem-cell procedure at UCLA Medical

Center and was almost miraculously cured of the disease. That experience, followed by a second cancer, and then later the death of his wife, have had a powerful impact on his life perspective, leading him to focus even more intensely on helping others heal and grow emotionally.

Since retiring from private practice in 2014, Ken has been leading small groups of laypeople, helping them learn to do this dreamwork in their own lives and enabling them to help others heal and grow as well. He has found that one does not need a professional degree to do this because of its straightforward simplicity.

You may contact Ken by e-mail at schmidtmft@yahoo.com

www.ingramcontent.com/pod-product-compliance
Lightning Source LLC
Chambersburg PA
CBHW060453280326
41933CB00014B/2742